1

A Coaches Collaborative

Everything you need to know
to thrive in your coaching business

ISBN: 978-0-9976105-4-3

Published by Scorpio Press 2016

For bulk orders contact Scorpio Press at:
660-864-0274 or email kelly@scorpio.press

If you operate your own coaching business - whether online or in person - you know there is a lot to learn! Get a jumpstart on the big stuff with this book written in collaboration by 12 coaches across all markets. From money mindset to managing a team, this is THE manual for coaches. Here's what our readers are saying:

"I think this book seems like a very valuable tool for aspiring coaches. It covers every aspect of the profession and really shows how this is one profession that you can't practice if you don't have your own ducks in a row. If you're not authentic, at peace and together yourself, you will quickly be labeled a fraud and lose credibility. This book offers the tools to help coaches identify the needs of their clients and relate to them on a personal level with an individualized approach that can be implemented many different ways. Cool concept."
~S.B.

"The Team Management Chapter was an easy read and very informative. Being a loyal Tony Robbins follower, I was amazed that I had never heard of the assessment testing he provides. I was glad that it was included in the chapter along with other ways to learn more about yourself and your team member's strengths.
This book will be a great asset to new and seasoned coaches alike."
~E. Z.

"I LOVE THE CHAPTER on authenticity Katie. You can feel your energy, positivity and light through your words. You spread your message in your writing because it is so authentic and real and you embody your message in how you share it. The advice you gave was 100% spot on, a real foundation to kicking off ANY business- not only for healers. This is a constant theme throughout the entire book… genuine, intuitive and straight from the heart. I will definitely share this book with the entrepreneurs who are my clients. Thank you!"

~KS

Index

Tarryne West with *Self Care*..........11

Cherrise Boucher with *Practical Magic*..........25

Dana Croy with *Personal Connections*..........43

Bonnie Chase, RN with *The Divine Feminine*...54

Katie Henry with *Follow Your Intuition*..........66

Melissa Kirkpatrick with *Find Your Drive*.....82

Annika Suoma Frey with *Everyday Tips & Tricks*.95

Kavita Singh with *Intuition & Change*..........110

Misti Patrella with *Money Mindset*.................119

Carla Gibson with *Be Your Own Client*.........133

Patti O'Leary with *Team Management*..........144

Aliza Bloom Robinson with *Saving Your Soul*....161

Resources......176

Website: http://tarrynewest.com
Instagram: @tarryne_west
Facebook: https://www.facebook.com/tarrynewest

Hi I'm Tarryne, and I help people to become healthier, happier and more successful as a personal development and wellness coach. I know seems like an odd combination, but in the years since I became a coach I've found that the two are inextricably linked.

Whether I'm supporting someone through losing 50 pounds - so that they actually feel like themselves and aren't held hostage by diet - or empowering them to be able to step away from the drama of stressful and anxious situations - so that they can get ahead in life without burnout or melt downs; I focus on the individual. I provide real life, practical tips, support and coping mechanisms. Everything I do is focused towards improved health and happiness.

Though I did formal study to become a coach at a University in New Zealand; my greatest learning experience has been using the principles behind coaching and self-care to free myself from major depression and a number of years of disordered eating. These same tools are what I use every day in my business as a professional coach with the freedom to choose my own clients and projects. More than a decade after I believed that depression was my future, my life and my work as a coach is now incredibly fulfilling, shared with a husband, a teenager and two insane rescued Chihuahuas all running around our own country home paradise in Texas.

Self-Care
Is The Life Of Your Business

by Tarryne West

When you're starting out in your own business, you're on a massive rolling ball of excitement, ideas, and extremely hard work. As a new coach, I think it's doubly so as most small coaching businesses are a one-man-band. You're doing everything from marketing to coaching, accounting and website work. You are IT, and if you're anything like I was, you're frantically trying to make headway and get your business booming!

The last thing that a new business owner and coach is generally thinking is "gosh I should really say no to this project, and instead take a day to breathe, eat well and go see my chiropractor... " But the truth is, it should be. I've learned in my own journey as a coach over the last 5 years that your self-care IS the LIFE of your business.

Self-care is an incredibly important aspect of my life because it was the catalyst that helped me free myself from major depression. I suffered from depression for 7 years that left me housebound for more than two of those. And it very nearly claimed my life. Implementing self- care changed my incredibly destructive relationship with food and my body. It changed how I thought about myself and what I believed I was capable of.

I'm not exaggerating when I say that it changed my life and its the reason that I became a coach.

It took me a little while to really "get" the lesson, though, because even after that incredible turnaround, I ignored what I'd gone through when it came to my business.

When I started coaching I regularly felt like a fraud. I was still working while doing a university level coaching qualification in my spare time and fitting in sessions with clients whenever I could. I was regularly overwhelmed and so exhausted that I'd often end up in tears. I remember one morning as I prepared to give a two-day workshop on self-image, wondering frantically if my clients would be able to tell that I hadn't slept in days. I was a disaster, but because I was a coach I kept up the whole "Oh yeah I got this. I'm a coach you know, I can do all the things and never sleep again."

No, I really couldn't. And as a result of two years of that nonsense, I did eventually burn out and I took my thyroid down with me.

During those two years, though, I was doing all the right things. At least I thought I was. I had read a thousand of those self-care lists, had green smoothies every day and worked out a LOT and I somehow managed to add a yoga practice into the aforementioned insane schedule. I was so zen it hurt. Right up until I really really wasn't zen anymore! I was so wrapped up in doing the stuff to really stop and consider if I was actually doing myself any good!

Self-care is not about what you do or even don't do. Real self-care is about letting go of expectations. Of allowing yourself space to really BE ok. And above all else. Self-care is about self-respect.

Coaching attracts a very particular type of person. We tend to be very focused, very driven and more often than not, selfless. Most coaches have a terrible habit of putting everyone and everything else first because we're too busy trying to change the world. Particularly as a new coach, it's easy to get so swept up in all the STUFF that you forget yourself. Coupled with the all or nothing, "do ALL the things" mentality that is so typical of the one-man-band coaching business, it's only a matter of time before burnout and exhaustion hits.

There are two distinct aspects to self-care for the coach, one very much about the business, the other is far more personal, but IS the business. because at the end of the day, no matter how you approach your work or marketing or niche... YOU ARE YOUR BUSINESS. Not just a resource, but everything you are as a person is a part of who you are as a coach.

Self-care for a coach means being your own client first and helping you do the best for YOU, no matter what that looks like.

Where to start…

Part of your work as a coach is to explore what your client is really looking for and the same exploration holds true for anything that you do for yourself as well. With that in mind, the goal of self-care becomes pretty simple. You want to be a great coach and help people. Right? In order to facilitate this in your clients, you have to be functional and in a good space yourself.

At the heart of it all, I believe that there are only two key elements to being an effective and functional person or coach.

1. Care for your body - As the saying goes, "It's the only one you've got."
2. Do the inner work - effective coaching is impossible without a deep level of emotional and mental wellness.

These two aspects of self-care are absolutely intertwined. One affects and influences the other. You can also only have one off balance for so long before the other starts to fail too. Both are essential for the coach, but luckily you have a world of resources at your fingertips to ensure you find the right mix of strategies to help YOU be the best, most highly functioning and happy YOU.

Free the body and the mind will follow…

Based on my personal experience and my work with helping others to create the same experience for themselves, I've come to believe that the body is the first and simplest place to start when it comes to your self-care. Your body is the vehicle that carries you around and gets you through this life and although your consciousness is not your body, they are linked and influence each other in ways that we are only just beginning to understand. Whether you take a scientific or spiritual approach to it (and I encourage both) the outcome is the same: Your body cannot escape your mind, and the mind is most definitely held accountable by your body.

Think about this like a business owner for a moment. Let's say that your business is 100% reliant on you having a car, so you buy yourself a great new car and you're happily running your business. Let's also say that you run that car for 18 hours a day, you don't use the correct gas and you completely neglect the maintenance of it.

Pretty soon, that engine is going to blow up and you'll be stuck sitting on the side of the road waiting for help and your business has ground to a screeching halt.

To be very straightforward, you HAVE to make sure you allocate time to keep yourself well and functional. There can be no compromising here! I can almost hear the protests already because I know that you're working your butt off trying to grow or launch your coaching business. And I also know you believe you need to burn up all the hours you can to accomplish that. Trust me when I tell you that no business is worth sacrificing your health and happiness for. That is part of the value system of what we teach our clients, so you need to live that.

Plus, you're a coach. So let's get smart about it and prioritize the basics. You can add in beach vacations and daily massages later on!

Being tired is not a sign of success…

Thankfully the days of bragging about how tired you are because you're just sooo busy and sooo super important at work are gone. Whose idea was it to make being a tired, brain-dead zombie a sign that you're succeeding at life? Being permanently tired is not only a terrible drain on your health but staying up all hours of the night to work is also a very poor business strategy. Thankfully, most people are starting to question the wisdom of exhaustion somehow being a sign of success.

A simple way to illustrate this is to think about the decisions you make when you're tired.

Are they the clearest, most effective decisions you've ever made? I'll bet not.

When you're physically tired you are simply not

capable of functioning mentally the way you would when you're rested. Research has shown that there is very little difference between tiredness and drunkenness when it comes to cognitive function.

Think about that for a moment... would you turn up and run your business or see clients when you're drunk?

I didn't think so...

Good sleep comes from a combination of routine and insuring your sleep is restful enough to be effective. Mentally your brain consolidates memories and puzzles over things you're working on. After a good rest you will think more clearly and have a better handle on the information you absorbed the day before.

Your body also does a great deal of clean up and rebuilding while you sleep. This includes the producing and regulating on a number of vital hormones, like cortisol. Cortisol is responsible not only for helping you actually get up and get going. If its out of balance it can absolutely ruin your ability to function and get through the day.

Sleep is absolutely foundational to self-care so you need to be certain to prioritize it. Like anything else, you need to personalize in order to get the best results, so experiment. Figure out what prevents you from having better sleep and work on creating simple routines to protect your sleep time. Whether that's something like journaling or meditating before bed to help shut your mind down, or simply being very strict with bedtime and turning off your devices. Whatever works for you, do it!

Health is not about body size…

While many of my clients come to me to lose weight, they discover very quickly that I have ulterior motives. I want to change their health.

I am a firm believer that if you give the body the right tools and environment, it will take care of the weight by itself. I also think the fixation on size as the only indicator of your health has caused far more problems than it's ever solved.

As a coach, whatever your goals are, you need your body to function as well as it can, or you'll never keep up with the demands of running a business - especially one as draining as coaching can be. You'll be less likely to recover quickly if you do get ill or need down time.

The field of nutrition and diet is vast and filled with conflicting information so I'm not going to go into much detail or prescribe to you how you should eat. What I am going to encourage you to do though is to think for yourself and do your own research. The biggest issue with nutrition is that there's a "one size fits all" mentality that does far more harm than good. Certainly our nutrition habits have a very big impact on your ability to successfully run a business, and be happy doing it.

Everyone's body, circumstances, hormonal balance, schedule, and tastes are unique. While there are some basic rules that are worth following, you have to experiment with what makes you feel your best and find what works for you.

The basic framework that I have found works for me and for most of my clients is this:

Eat real food.
There are countless books out there discussing the extremely detrimental impact that processed food has on our bodies. If you do nothing else, simply making the majority of your day to day food real and unprocessed will have a massive positive effect.

Balance.
In my experience, any kind of extreme is going to create issues. As long as your daily nutritional habits are good, the occasional treats are not going to matter. Life is too short to fear having a glass of wine or an enormous slice of cheesecake. Balance is also good for mental health. Being a hostage to your diet, even if it's a nutritionally good diet, is not going to create a healthy mindset.

Listen to your body.
If you listen to your body carefully, there is no greater source of information on this subject than your own body. With every change you make, pay

attention. What are your energy levels like? What is your digestion like? How do you feel? Each of us has a unique body that responds in its own way to how we treat it. By experimenting with your daily nutrition and listening carefully for the response, your body will tell you exactly what you need and how much is right for you.

Do the inner work…

While I would say that all of the aspects of self-care are important, I believe that they are simply band-aids without having done your own inner work.

Recently a friend who is in the process of starting her own business asked me if I had any advice. I told her that she was about to do something that was going to bring up every fear, insecurity and dysfunctional belief system she had and that she needed to be ready to work through these things when they surfaced or they would sabotage her business success.

Within days she was calling me going "OMG you were so right! How do I deal with this stuff?!"

As a coach running your own business, this is even more of a factor because you're not just a business person, you're doing work which is deeply connected to your own understanding of who you are, who you want to be and your very purpose. There is a great deal of fear and potentially destructive beliefs around those things for any normal person and when it becomes something you charge people money for, it's a potential landmine.

Doing the inner work means treating yourself like your most valued client.

Whatever your particular focus as a coach, you're going to work through the same goal setting process that you facilitate with your clients. You're going to face issues with procrastination, time management, and motivation. You need to put together a solid action plan for how you're going to manage yourself through these. Running a business and being a coach is going to bring you experiences that will challenge you and will bring you the opportunities to face who you are underneath it all. From your business strategy to the content you create, each will bring up a moment of fear. If I think of the number of times I've stopped short at an opportunity and thought "Who do I think I am to be doing this? No one's going to listen to me, what do I know?!" I'm blown away by how much time I've wasted.

Luckily, you don't need to do that. No one told me when I started out that every time I published a blog post I would wonder if anyone was ever going to bother reading it. Or that I would have moments where I was struck numb by fear every time I booked a client, terrified that I wouldn't be able to help them and would have no idea what to do.

No one ever told me that when I lost a client I was going to question everything I've ever done and started searching online for a job!

If you do the work and face head on everything that this calling throws at you, these things fade and quickly. No matter how far along your own development journey you go, you have to remember that no one is or will ever be perfect. You will always be a work in progress, just like your clients. And just because you are the coach does not mean you have to have it all figured out. It just means that you're further down the path than your clients are!

Doing the inner work is a matter of integrity too. Everything that we share with and coach our clients on, we need to have experienced and be fully invested in. If you're not working with your own fears and limitations, you will be missing a powerful element of your work that could mean the difference between being a good coach and being a life changing one.

Most importantly, however, is that doing the inner work gives you the tools to create a life that is the right one for you. There is nothing to be gained from chasing success or building a business if you're unhappy, unfocused and operating out of fear. Be your own client first, work with a coach of your own. Do what you need to do in order to prioritize your self-care.

Cherrise Boucher

Get my planner here: www.cherriseboucher.com

Get a free 30-minute session:
www.cherriseboucher.com/ schedule

Facebook: www.facebook.com/cdboucher1

Instagram: @cherrisedboucher

Get my training *5 Steps to Get Shit Done & Reach Your Biz Goals EVERY TIME* here:

http://www.cherriseboucher.com/5-steps-to-get-shit-done

I am Cherrise Boucher and I am a Momentum Strategist. I focus on helping smart, sassy, driven women go from that place of overwhelm and mind clutter, where procrastination lives, to having clarity in the steps they need to move forward.

I grew up on the coast of southern Maine and have lived in Florida for more than half my life now. I've discovered that the ocean is my compass and I can't live too far from the coast because I have no idea which direction I'm going when I do! I am a mom to two awesome teenagers and create balance in my life by going on nature hikes, reading in my hammock, and creating business momentum in my outside workspace.

My passion lies in getting what's inside your head, your big vision, projects, brilliant ideas, out on paper and planned out perfectly so your next steps are easy, clear and actionable. We collaborate so that all the pieces fit together and the 'how's' aren't elusive anymore.

When we work together, time becomes your friend because you aren't wasting it on THINKING about what to do, YOU ARE DOING it! "Get Shit Done" is my motto and baby... do we ever!

Practical Magic

by Cherrise Boucher

I make sure to bring awareness and energy management into my work and encourage people to practice this daily. Yes, what some may consider that woo woo stuff seriously creates a sense of peace and greatly helps reduce stress in your business and life.

That being said, I chose to write this chapter because I think I'm a pretty practical person. I help others with practical approaches to their lives and businesses, I think spatially, and can envision next step processes in a rational manner. But I am in no way a stiff. I'm very laid back, I'm sassy and I'm not afraid to swear. When I started to outline what I would include under this Practical Magic umbrella I discovered that it encompasses way more than I anticipated and it made me realize I've learned more than I thought over the the past years. There are so many processes and practices that I've played with, implemented and now teach, that I want to share with you. (The fact that the movie Practical Magic with Sandra Bullock and Nicole Kidman pops up in my head when I think about this chapter makes me happy too!).

The entire basis of everything I talk about and teach is Awareness. When you become very familiar with this concept change is so much easier.

And boy do I wish I had known this YEARS ago! Change can be a simple shift in perspective, routine, habits or thoughts. Very simple, very specific, very doable. Let's begin with 5 Simple Practical Magic Guidelines and some practical tips to implement along the way.

Practical Mindset

New coaches, myself included, experience a range of emotions when beginning the journey. Excitement about a new venture, apprehension about learning a lot of new stuff, nervousness about talking to clients, self-doubt around the… who am I to do this? topic. So being aware of where your mind is going and what you are telling yourself is key to staying on track and minimizing deflation.

Be ok with where you are right now.

This is super, super, super important! Everyone starts at the same place, the beginning. But you will never get where you envision yourself if you don't begin and stay the course. So get comfortable with being uncomfortable and put your learning cap on.

Tip: Write yourself a love note and place it in a place you will see throughout the day saying, "I am exactly where I should be right now." And give yourself permission to be ok with that.

Give yourself permission to ask for help.

You are not alone in this journey. Don't think you need to start from scratch and make it all up on your own. ASK FOR HELP. I can't stress this enough. If you are anything like me this can be a tough one to move past. Any of these sound familiar?

If you want it done right you better do it yourself.

It's easier to just do it myself rather than take the time to explain it to someone else.

I'm a smart woman, I can totally figure this out on my own.

I'll be bothering people if I ask for help.

I get it, but I'm telling you right now that you are wrong. There are so many people out there, including myself, who are willing to help. But you have to reach out and ask.

Tip: Write a note and place it on your mirror, computer or wherever you will see it frequently throughout your day that says, "I give myself permission to ask for help when I need it." Consider saying this as an affirmation. Affirmations are so awesome that I've created three decks of them for people to use in their daily awareness practice.

Be AWARE of when you find yourself stuck on something or spending too much time searching for an answer. This is a sign that you need to ask for assistance. Getting involved in Facebook groups with other people who are on the same path as you is a great way to make connections. Start compiling a list of people who specialize in different areas so you can create your own resource directory. Ask for recommendations - everybody knows somebody.

Tip: Start a spreadsheet or document listing people who are recommended to you or that you find on your own who specialize in different areas of expertise. This can be your go-to resource when you need help with something.

Stop trying to be the dictator of time.

When you find yourself thinking that something is taking much longer than you anticipated, realize that everything happens in its own time, customized especially for you. Yup, this is a challenge too. We all want things to happen yesterday. Everything I'm sharing with you here is something I have or still go through. There are some difficult things to consider sometimes, things we don't really want to look at but have to. Nobody likes to call themselves out on their own shit. But the sooner you start opening your eyes to it the faster you can move forward.

If you are getting frustrated with the less-than-warp-speed results of building your business, take a good hard look and ask yourself if you are doing EVERYTHING you can to move forward. This is best done with another person to brainstorm with and who will ask you the tough questions you will have to answer. Like a coach! More likely than not you will discover some blocks, things you don't like to do or have resisted in the past, maybe you'll uncover some things you have not even considered before.

Again, awareness of what is holding you back will help you overcome it and move forward.

Tip: Get a coach. I don't know of any successful coaches who don't have a coach of their own that helps them uncover blocks, set goals, brainstorm ideas, and set action steps. This will inevitably help you gain traction and provide the accountability needed to keep moving forward.

Be aware of beliefs that pop up and try to hold you back.

Those good ol' limiting beliefs as they are called in the industry. These are not the I can do anything I set my mind to beliefs, these are the I don't know enough to help others or I'm not good enough beliefs that like to fester in your mind. They pop up just when you are ready to offer something to someone, create a webinar, or announce a new program. Things like:

We aren't comfortable putting ourselves out there, this doesn't feel safe.

They say and do their damndest to keep you in your comfort zone. We've all the heard the saying Growth doesn't happen in your comfort zone, and it is 100% true. You need to be aware of when this happens so you can counteract it, swat these mistaken beliefs like flies and keep going forward.

Tip: When limiting beliefs pop up, think about a time when you felt the same way but had a positive outcome. It doesn't have to be a same situation type of thing, just a time when you felt the same. When you pushed through and you felt amazing afterward or maybe you felt accomplished and successful. Use this as ammunition against those crappy beliefs that try to hold you back.

Practical Learning

There will be a fair share of learning on this coaching journey. And you will be super excited at the beginning, like a sponge wanting to soak up every bit of new information, techniques and tools you come across. That is awesome! Learn away my friend! But be aware if you find yourself signing up for too many freebies or courses to just learn just one more thing. This often becomes a form of procrastination. Ongoing learning but not applying it is procrastination in its finest. It becomes an excuse for not putting yourself out there. Don't do this.

You will hear over and over again that you only need to be a few steps ahead of someone else to help them. Think about this. When you were in the second grade and had younger siblings or friends didn't you help them learn things you had already learned? I know I did. I even helped friends with things we were currently learning if it was something I was grasping quickly. I'm sure you can go back to elementary school and think of several instances where you did exactly this. Right now is no different. Whatever you have learned is something you can help someone else with. A good way to practice this is to keep your eye out for social media posts where someone may be asking for feedback or help on something you are good at or have learned a thing or two about. Help them out. This boosts your confidence level and starts letting people know that you have experience around this thing and maybe you'll end up on their resource list!

Absolutely keep learning while on your journey. You will discover all kinds of new things that you can implement into your own coaching. Just do it concurrently with getting out and moving forward in your business. Be aware of learning potentially becoming an excuse or a way to procrastinate and catch it mid-flight. When you become aware of these subtle signs of ways you may potentially hold yourself back you will be able to shift very quickly into action.

Tip: Build your confidence in what you already know by helping others seeking advice, feedback or help.

Practical Systems and Practices

You may already be awesome at organizing and implementing processes. For many of us starting new habits, even goods ones, can be a little difficult. I'm not talking about buying pretty journals, folders and colorful pens (though that is totally fun to do)! What I want to encourage is setting up helpful systems right at the beginning. The sooner you set up some simple processes the better. As your business grows you will already have things in place to keep you on track and it is much easier to get into good business habits when things are slower and in the beginning stages than later on when you are crazy busy with clients.

Let's talk about you first. Women are notorious for putting themselves last. No more, ladies! Here's how we are going to do this so you are scheduling yourself into your own life. Taking care of yourself and managing your energy are critical to the success of your business.

Think of things that you can do every day that will allow you to check off the self-care box on your to-do list. Here are a few suggestions: walking, jogging, yoga, reading, meditating, intentional breathing, working out, dancing, playing an instrument, taking a long hot bath or shower, swimming even taking a short nap. You don't have to schedule a day at the spa for things to be considered self-care, but by all means do that if you like! You can even reward yourself with extra special self-care when you have completed goals if that is something that motivates you.

Tip: Motivate yourself with a reward of something you really enjoy when you have completed a goal.

Make sure you do something for you EVERY DAY.

Actually include it on your calendar if you have to. The intention is not for it to be complicated or a chore. Simply being aware (yup, there it is again) of what your body is telling you will trigger what I like to call an energy reset. Pay attention to fatigue, tension within your body, irritability or even when things are just not going right like you can't complete a simple task or you find yourself making excessive typing errors. These are signs that it is time for an energy reset. A very simple way to do this is to stop what you are doing, go outside if you can, if you can't at least get up and move to a different location, plant your feet firmly on the ground and become very present. Take a few deep breaths, holding each for a few seconds, and as you release visualize all tension, negativity and stuck energy moving down through your body and being released into the earth through the soles of your feet. Be very in the moment when you are doing this.

Tip: Practice energy resets throughout the day. *Be aware of signs such as tension, irritability, fatigue or things generally not going right (ongoing tech issues, anyone?) and take it as a sign to take a little break. You can do one of your self-care activities or you can do this quick reset. Go outside, take your shoes off and plant your feet firmly on the ground. Become very present within your body and your surroundings. Take a few deep breaths, holding each for a few seconds and as you release visualize all tension, stuck energy and negativity moving down through your body and being released into the earth through the soles of your feet. It's amazing how good you will feel when you practice this!*

Implement some strategic planning.

This is my area of expertise. Part of the results of working with me are walking away with an actionable roadmap. I did a training on this where I literally laid out the first steps I take with my clients. This was the "5 Steps to Get Shit Done and Reach Your Biz Goals EVERY Time" training. In it I suggest you sit down and brain-dump what you would like to do and accomplish. List it all. Go back through each item and further list sub-items associated with it. Prioritize everything set deadlines and then action steps on your calendar to accomplish everything on your list. I've created a simple planner that is totally free to download that you may find useful in your weekly planning process. It provides some prompts and guidance on how to effectively plan and makes sure you don't skip out on taking care of yourself. You can get it on my website (the link is back there with my name and photo!).

I know this sounds simple and I realize that this is easier said than done. And that's where asking for help comes in. Whether you work with me or someone else, it really helps to brainstorm with another person because brilliant plans and ideas are often developed when people get in a space of collaboration. Many people find it easier to talk it out than to just sit and plan. I work with many clients who like to work this way. Personally I find myself doing laundry or scrubbing a toilet instead of planning. It's not the most fun business thing you can do that's why it helps to have someone hold you accountable for setting the time aside to do it and to making sure you stay on track.

Tip: Accountability partners are great! Have someone to help you brainstorm, plan and then hold each other accountable for taking action.

Practical Action-Taking

Becoming overwhelmed at various points along the way are inevitable. When you start noticing that you are doing less and less meaningful and potentially income-producing activities you need to revisit your plan. If you are unclear on exactly how to reach a goal or accomplish a project you have an idea for, get help. Are you noticing a couple themes here? My clients have a working outline of everything they want to do or create. This outline is broken down into actionable steps to keep them moving forward. If you don't have something like this you should seriously consider creating one. With each project outlined it is easy to see what you need to do to keep it moving forward.

Consistently taking action is the key to momentum.

It seems to be a simple concept yet getting stuck in figuring out the most efficient and effective actions can be a challenge for even the most seasoned entrepreneurs. If you feel like the days just fly by and you aren't getting key things done or if you are not increasing your direct interaction with potential clients, then you need to revisit what you are doing and consider what meaningful actions you can implement.

Are you putting offers out to talk with potential clients, solving a problem for them that they have been struggling with? Are you getting out there in your community and sharing what you do? Are you increasing visibility online by guest blogging, writing articles, being interviewed on podcasts or other interview series? Are you saying YES to opportunities when they come your way?

Tip: Make a list of activities you can do that will get you in front of potential clients. Think both locally and online. Keep this list handy and add to it as more things come to mind. Refer back to this list whenever you are feeling a slump in your visibility and interaction with potential clients. Then make sure you take action on at least one every day.

Practical Things To Be Aware Of

I'd like to wrap up this chapter with a few things to keep in mind no matter what stage you are in of your coaching career.

Energy and time, leaks and drainers.

These are things that you can literally feel are sucking the energy (and time) right out of you. Too much time spent on social media is a big one. Feeding into drama is another. Awareness can solve both of these issues and more. Creating a schedule for yourself that allots specific time blocks for social media can help you manage this time. If you find yourself wasting time and energy in areas that are not meaningfully productive, a schedule that you can stick to is an awesome tool. Another great tool that can be used in a million ways is the Pomodoro Technique ®. If you haven't heard of it let me give you the very simple down and dirty of this time-saving method for productivity developed by Francesco Cirillo. It promotes single-tasking, which really is the only way to actually get things done efficiently. I know many of us pride ourselves on multi-tasking and this mindset really needs to shift.

All that is required to be successful with this technique is a list of things you would like to do and a timer. Select one item on your list, set the timer (you can use the one on your phone) for 25 minutes and work diligently on that one task. When the timer goes off, take a 5 minute break setting the timer so you don't go over. Do anything during this 5 minutes. Come back, set the timer for another 25 minutes. After you have finished four of these 25 minute blocks of time you can give yourself a longer 20-30 minute break. This method couldn't be simpler and you'll find you accomplish more than you thought you would - guaranteed!

Tip: Practice the Pomodoro Technique® for efficient time and energy saving ways to get stuff done.

As for time and energy sucking drama, be aware of when you are falling into it. Then quickly shift gears, do an energy reset, reframe your thinking and take yourself out of the situation. You'll be glad you did!

Comparisonitis is something we all fall victim to at one point in time or another. You start looking at other people's websites, how successful they are, how many followers they have, etc. and start feeling bad for where you are. Please don't do this. Like I mentioned earlier, everyone started at the beginning. Be aware of when this is showing up for you and remind yourself that you are well on your way, you are taking action, and you are exactly where you should be right now. If you feel unclear about the next steps you should be taking or need clarity around an idea and how you can move forward with it, ask for help! As you know, I am pretty damn good at getting this stuff out of your head and into action. And most of my clients get more out of an idea than they even considered possible once we have worked together.

Shiny object syndrome is a buzzword in the coaching industry. It's a phrase you'll hear it a lot.

You are a victim of this affliction if you find yourself signing up for every program, course and free offering you can get your hands on. Your reasoning is that THIS thing is what you need to really kick start your business. You just need to learn this ONE additional thing and then you'll be ready to go. Procrastination at it's finest. Remember earlier I mentioned how you can teach those a few steps behind you? You will grow and learn as your business grows. Don't overwhelm yourself with more courses and information. Get out there and take action.

Tip: Celebrate what you are good at! Acknowledge it and give yourself the credit you deserve. You know what you are doing so share it with people who can benefit from it.

Self-sabotage happens to the best of us. Be conscious of what you are saying to yourself. This falls in line with everything I've discussed in this chapter. If you feel that you are getting into some negative self-talk intentionally shift it. Reflect on something you are brilliant at and how that makes you feel. If you don't necessarily think you are brilliant at anything ask someone else to tell you what you are good at. Other people know better than you do. We take what we are good for granted because it usually comes easy to us and we think everyone can do it. Not so. Give yourself credit for your gifts and pat yourself on the back for being so good at them!

Be aware of what you think about and say to yourself. If it isn't all positive change it! Don't let yourself get in your way. That is all too often what happens with entrepreneurs and they give up too quickly. You never know how close you are to success until you have reached it. You won't see how all the steps you have taken and how all the changes in direction were exactly the right moves until you get to where to want to go. Don't give up too soon. Stay the course and follow your heart and vision. This journey and career takes a strong level of belief, faith, trust and motivation. You can do it! Awareness, asking for help and establishing good practices in the beginning will build a solid foundation for you to build a business you are passionate about!

Dana Croy

Website: http://www.danacroy.com

Facebook: www.facebook.com/iamfengshuimama

Twitter: @danacroy

Instagram: @fengshuimama

I'm Dana Croy — Feng Shui Mama with an emphasis on the Mama. This life has been filled with many teachers, wild women, and shaman who took me into their sacred circles and have assisted me in finding a deeper understanding of myself, the world around me and the heavens above. That journey, begun over twenty years ago, led me to both Reiki and Feng Shui certifications which combined with my professional background in non-profit development and retail management has allowed me to create a heart-centered business. Through this lens, I offer Sacred Space Clearing, Decluttering Services and Coaching for other heart-centered entrepreneurs. My hubby and I call Nashville, Tennessee home and are parents of two children who constantly remind us how unenlightened we truly are. When not working with clients or driving the kids around in the family taxi I am teaching—online, and around Nashville.

Let's Get Personal

Interpersonal Relationships Are The Keys to Building Your Coaching Business

*We have a primal need for story,
and it is through the sharing of those stories that
relationships are built. - Dana Croy*

As coaches, one fantastic thing we bring to the table is a story. We coach from our story. And that, my friends, is a true story. Here is mine:

Before launching my coaching business, my professional background was a journey through retail management, non-profit development, and fundraising with a liberal dose of volunteerism and board service mixed in. To some, the retail and non-profit fields do not entirely mesh. In reality, they not only mesh, they also go hand-in-hand in how clients are served. They have both taught me many valuable lessons that I apply to my coaching business each and every day. Through all of these professional gigs, I always had a side business, and, though always somewhat successful, I knew something was missing. Eventually, I came to a place where I needed to get off the wheel. I pulled the kids from school, and for a year, we homeschooled, spent lots of time with family, did a little traveling and, in general, got a clearer picture of where we were headed. I realized that while I was capable of being an entrepreneur, there was only one thing I could sell—myself. But, which one of my gifts could I offer to my clients?

I have something to share, but I don't know what it is.

So, you want to coach. Do you know what you are sharing? When you sit down with a client, what are you coaching them toward? For many of us who begin on this path, we simply do not know where our gifts lie. We are good at a lot of things. Our heart is filled with the desire to serve. But, in what way? Trust me, I speak from experience. Though I had always known the answers to what my gifts were, it took that year off for me to pull what I could share and how I could coach together in a cohesive package. This is where interpersonal relationships come in.

If you are like me (and I suspect many coaches are), you are the go-to girl. For me, I have been the go-to-girl for friends and family in regards to home (Feng Shui and clutter clearing), parenting and education (do you see a theme?), and small business support (thanks largely to my retail background). My phone rang so often, I received so many emails and so many people showed up at my door or took me out for coffee or asked for help, that my husband began to ask me what I was charging.

What?

In his world, the IT realm, the service I offered to friends and family is called "consulting" and folks are paid big money for that time and attention. I told myself, "I could never do that. My services aren't valuable. No one will pay me for that." WRONG! It took many years for me to break myself of that mindset. It took many years of self-study and going to the mountain to understand that I have been building face to face relationships which had the potential to launch me into business. It took getting off that wheel for a full year to see the path ahead.

Don't get me wrong. I do the online thing. But, I also spend a large portion of my time reaching out to friends and family for referrals, networking and coaching face to face, which will allow me to have both repeat clients as well as word of mouth clients. This is when those go-to-girl freebie sessions in my past begin to serve the business of my present and future.

Relationships are the key to life.

That was how my LinkedIn profile looked—until recently. Why did I change it? It was not reflective of my business and the services that I offer, but it was reflective of my approach to clients and, just as equally, life. My many years in retail taught me how to approach clients (customers), ask open ended questions to ascertain their needs and then, close the sale. While still in retail, I took first a volunteer position, then a board seat and finally a full-time paid position as the primary fundraiser for a private school in Nashville, where my family and I reside.

Those relationship building skills—those people muscles—that I developed in retail became crucial in the quest to raise money, bringing meaningful education to children each and every day. Through the course of my time at the school, I was either part of a team or a one-woman show, instrumental in raising nearly a million dollars over six years. That was not accomplished through sending emails or letters. Well, there was some of that, but the bulk of the money raised by my team or by me was through direct, face-to-face, relationship building.

I still use those relationship tools in acquiring clients and in my coaching.

We live in a digital age. I get it. There are people making millions via affiliate links, emails with Buy Now buttons, downloads and more. I know. But, the key to building your coaching platform when starting out is the face to face—the interpersonal relationships that drive your business which is then shared with others.

Let me tell you a story (or two).

If you are still not sure if relationship building is where it is at, read on. When I decided to hang my shingle (gulp), the Universe put a local metaphysical fair right in front of me as an opportunity to meet some of the folks that are part of my target market. I took a huge leap of faith and contacted the owner of the event to ask if I could put a flyer in her program. Guess what? She never responded. I was not finished. I emailed her again. Nothing. There is something in addition to relationships that is the key to life.

P-E-R-S-I-S-T-E-N-C-E

Later in the week, I stopped by the local new age store. While chatting with the owner—a long- time acquaintance—I asked if he had ever attended this particular event. By the end of the conversation, he had texted his good friend—the owner of the event —and secured a spot for my flyer. That in turn led to my first two clients and recurring business from both. Those clients, that launch, was directly related to the relationship I had built with that person through the years.

This thread has repeated itself over and over as I have built my coaching business. I've shared my first story, and now as a bookend, I want to share my most recent win. As a busy mom, much of my business is centered around my children's schedules which means that during the summer, I take fewer clients. Summer break is coming to a close and to ensure that I have clients lined up, I sent personalized emails to every realtor in my personal address book (no spamming allowed) and within two hours, I had an invitation from one contact to attend a networking event as her guest with the promise of booking a future session for herself. These are relationships I have fostered, in one way or another, throughout the years, including sending client referrals to them, and there is no doubt in my mind that these will continue to give me a fantastic return on that relationship investment.

Can you build your coaching business through virtual relationships?

In other words, can you build a coaching business entirely online with no in-person, face to face or interpersonal interaction? Every coach needs to find the answer to this within themselves. For me, the answer is no, but I personally thrive on the face-to-face. And, it is through those clients and their testimonials that my entire business (real and virtual) is being built.

There are many coaches who have built stellar businesses in the virtual world, and with today's technology, we can easily access those who want to work with us from miles away. One of my coaching services is clearing both the physical space and the energetic space. Both of these often center around frank discussions of why the clutter or energy is hanging around like a favorite pet. And, both can be done virtually or remotely. Technology allows me to speak with people via Skype, Facebook Messenger, Google Hangouts, and ways that I am sure I am not even aware of. If your means of remote coaching involve a phone call or video, coaching remains personal despite great distances.

Remember those successful online coaches I was talking about earlier? Did those coaches begin online, or was virtual coaching a natural progression? Do those coaches see both in person and virtual clients? Chances are, those coaches began by building face-to-face programs as a model, building their client base, growing their testimonials and credibility which led them to build their online business. Consider this: Most of the truly successful coaches out there, regardless of the field, still offer one-on-ones or have a team of trained coaches surrounding them available to offer that service.

You prefer group dynamics to one-on-one. Is this still interpersonal? It depends.

Maybe you have seen transformation for clients while in a group setting. Maybe working with individual clients makes you uncomfortable. Maybe you are in an industry serving clients who themselves are uncomfortable with individual sessions. I get that. In fact, the next coach I will be hiring (yes, even coaches get coached) does a significant portion of her work virtually and on group calls, with a few one-on-ones and even a retreat thrown in. Each coach has to decide how to make their business work, serve the needs of their clients, and support their needs in the process.

Whether or not you can build relationships that way will depend on factors such as how you reach your clients, how large your group is, what the problem is that you are solving, and whether or not you offer additional in-person training. I know of one truly successful business coach with a seven-figure business (yes, I said seven-figures) whose coaching career began less than ten years ago progressed like this:

- In-person coaching

- Individual virtual coaching via phone, Skype, etc.

- Virtual group coaching

- Currently offering group coaching only (no individual) via a paid membership site (2,500+ members)

After a couple of years of the virtual group model, that coach realized something in her coaching was missing —not only for her clients but for herself as well. She now maintains her business with the group coaching via the membership site, but she has added a two-day free yearly retreat (travel/hotel not included) for any of her membership clients who can travel to her location.

She is a coaching rock star who realized there is value in sitting across with her clients to share her wisdom and expertise, and her business growth is reflective of that decision.

With that said, your target client may largely inform this decision. I am familiar with another coach who runs a virtual membership site (on a much smaller scale) for clients with extreme shyness who essentially never leave their homes. This seriously limits her ability to meet clients in an individual setting, and for her, virtual group coaching is where it's at!

It's up to you.

Each coach, each entrepreneur, has to make the decision how to serve their clients. In-person, individually, virtually, in a group setting, it's up to you. For me, speaking to potential clients, looking them in the eye, sharing my story and, more importantly, giving them the chance to share theirs, is the key to building a coaching business, having consistent clients and being of service in the way that my do-gooder's heart requires.

How do you want to be served? When building your coaching business, when thinking of those personal relationships, the question is what do you want in a coach?

- A great listener?

- A motivator?

- An expert in their field?

- A drill sergeant?

- An earth goddess? How do you want to be met?
- Over coffee?

- On the phone?

- In an office?

- Via Skype?

- Through a Facebook page?

Only you can answer these questions and a host of others which determine how your coaching business evolves. If you are struggling with the best way to serve your clients, to meet their needs, to build a relationship or rapport, look within yourself to see what would make your own heart sing. Look within to determine what would serve you best if the tables were turned, and you were the one seeking a coach.

On a final note.

There are no rights and wrongs as you build your coaching business. At least this is what I tell myself when I go to sleep each night. Look at who you are serving. Look at your gifts. Be persistent, build relationships and your coaching business will be a gift to the world.

Bonnie Chase RN

Website: www.bonniechase.com

Facebook: http://www.bit.ly/BonnieChase

http://www.facebook.com/CurvySisters

http://www.facebook.com/InspirewithDesireQuotes

Twitter: @bonniechasern

Bonnie Chase is a Holistic Registered Nurse, a Soul Centered Business Strategist and Coach, a Divine Feminine Living Alchemist, Foodie + Wine enthusiast! She is a woman who knows that red pumps and lip gloss aren't the only way to be feminine. Bonnie helps women create Soul-centered businesses infused with Divine Feminine Magic. She helps them break free from societal conditioning to find their authentic voice, monetize their message, and live their purpose while sharing their unique gifts in the world.

Divine Feminine Magic in Business

by Bonnie Chase

*"Owning your feminine essence creates an
abundant business and life"*
~ Bonnie Chase

Business has traditionally been a masculine
institution. Men run business, well, like men!
Masculine businesses thrive on competition,
thought, pressure, focus, demand, hard, strategic
and money energies. Masculine business follow
formulas, blueprints and strategies for growth.
When women work or operate their business with
these regimented and controlling energies, it leads
to imbalance, fatigue, burnout and job
dissatisfaction. Women do not thrive in a male
dominant or patriarchal environment. Women are
created differently than men and do much better
operating a business or working in businesses that
integrate the feminine. The time has come for
women to break free from the institution of
patriarchy and embrace the Divine Feminine as a
way of life.

The Divine Feminine or Goddess energy differs
from the masculine. Living and operating a

business with the Divine Feminine is about integrating the energy of collaboration, fairness, peace, nurturing, yielding, feeling, flowing, creation, intuition, balance, and abundance. The modern business woman who embraces her feminine nature brings more balance, collaboration and abundance to the coaching and business world.

The Dalai Lama quote, "the world will be saved by the Western woman," created quite a stir in the social media world. However, I believe this is only partially accurate.

The reality is, that the world will be saved by the spiritually conscious female entrepreneur who embraces the Divine Feminine.

Women naturally bring more love, nurturing and connection into their business and life. Women are heart centered and tend to focus more on being of service resulting in the change we want to see in the world.

When we look at the current trends of online businesses, most entrepreneurs use more masculine business techniques, including women. When I first began the journey into starting my online business, I used the same techniques to build my business. I followed someone's formula or blueprint to set up my ideal client, offerings and packages. My marketing and social media also followed a formula. The result, failure! I was not happy. I felt stifled and trapped in an uncomfortable place. My message felt forced and not authentic while I dutifully followed the business methods and formulas of several different business coaches. Even though my intuition kept telling me that something was not right, I ignored it. By ignoring my intuitive guidance, I pushed forward in a way that was out of alignment with my Soul. I spent hours working on my business without results. I just kept spinning my wheels. I made no progress. I was in a constant state of thinking, forcing, change and indecision. I became frustrated, confused and stagnant. Still... I knew there had to be a better way.

All women are blessed with an inner knowing and the ability to read between the lines. The trouble is we so often ignore our feminine intuition and follow the advice or direction of the business gurus or coaches in the online business world. I am no different. I've just about earned a master's degree in online business through the coaching and courses. I've spent close to $100,000 in my informal education!

In spite of the large investments I've made, I still felt something was missing.

For years, I've had this deep inner knowing that I have a big mission in the world to make a difference in the lives of millions of women. I spent years trying to figure out my ideal client avatar or defining my niche. I am a Registered Nurse with a holistic living philosophy. I became disillusioned by the conventional medical system and set out to help women heal their bodies through spiritual and mindset techniques. The typical business coach and traditional coaching and business methods didn't understand what I was trying to create and persuaded me to water my message down so I would not turn off clients. This only created confusion and indecision for me and halted progress in my business. Each direction I turned felt wrong. I couldn't move forward if it didn't feel right to me. What I learned was that by trying to avoid being a turn off to potential clients with my unorthodox message, I was turning them off because I was not being authentic. People can energetically sense when you are not in alignment with your message. Since I had a spiritual mission, my business needed to be Soul-aligned. I needed more than to simply make money, I needed to make a difference in the world.

There comes a time when you have to stop fighting. It was time for me to give up. Not give up my dream of having my own online business that would lead to financial freedom but giving up the techniques that did not feel good. The time had come to step out of the traditional business box. I stopped conforming to the traditional and masculine ways of business. I stopped trying to force my business in the traditional sense. Enough was enough. I turned inward and finally listened to my intuition.

Finally, I joined a women's mastermind group of spirit led entrepreneurs who spoke Goddess like I do. The sisterhood and support I received was invaluable for me to grow into the powerful woman that I am. I felt free to explore my theories and ideas in a safe, supportive, and sacred space. I started doing business with Soul. I was supported in turning inward and finally listen to my feminine intuition. Doors opened for me and the ideas flooded in. After years of trying to force myself into a business of healthy living and health coaching, I discovered the business I was meant to own. The one thing that I'd been pushing away and denying was the one thing I was meant to do in my business. Women came to me to help them with their businesses. I helped them with strategies to grow their business and set up programs and courses. They didn't come to me for health coaching or helping them to heal their body from disease. They came to me for business advice and strategies. I finally had to own my purpose. I help spiritual entrepreneurs and healers with their business and life strategy. I help them create businesses aligned with their Soul and support them to live their Goddess Life. My business now is deeply rooted in feminine principles, feeling and intuition. I believe that conscious, spirit led women will heal the state of business and it will change the world by integrating the Divine Feminine into their daily business. My new awakening was pure FREEDOM!

6 Principles of Divine Feminine Magic in Business:

When I began to follow my feminine guidance in business, I learned a new way to create abundance. The Divine Feminine in business is powerful and satisfying. In order for women to be happy and satisfied in business they need to become aligned to the Divine Feminine magic within. Women are here to be of service and nurture others into a greater sense of well-being. I have found that there are *6 Divine Feminine principles* to create joy and freedom in business.

Purpose

Women are not wired to just have a business. We must have a mission behind what we do each day. If we just go to work day to day and feel stagnant, we will be unhappy. We have to have a purpose to our lives and businesses. Each of us has our own unique Divine Purpose to fulfill during our lifetime. Our Divine Purpose is our Soul's mission during our lifetime. No two missions are the same. We each bring different skills, abilities and life experiences into our business that is influenced by what our Soul is here to learn. When deciding on the type of business, your niche, your ideal client, etc., keep your life purpose or the difference you want to make in the world at the forefront of your mind. When you align with your purpose, you will find business more satisfying. Finding our Divine purpose can sometimes seem to be a challenge. One thing to remember is that our biggest struggle is what we are here to teach.

Intuition

Women's intuition. Every woman possesses the gift of inner knowing or intuition, our internal guidance system. Women have the ability to read between the lines and tune into the energy of a situation. Men do not have this same ability. Women have a special gift. When women tap into their inner wisdom, they see clearly and far. What happens most often is that we deny the gut feelings or intuitive knowing that we get so our intuition slowly dims. We are able to wake up our intuition and strengthen it by listening and following to its guidance.

When we don't follow our intuition, we find ourselves running in circles, physically depleted, or in a business we don't enjoy. When making decisions, listening and feeling into intuitive guidance will bring you back into balance and into a greater knowing that's in alignment with your Soul. You are the Divine Feminine incarnate and hold an immense power within you to create the life and business that you desire. Following your intuition will bring you many abundant blessings.

Authenticity

Being authentic is part of our Divine Feminine Magic. Throughout life, women often defer to the needs, wants, desires, and our dreams of our families, friends and society. Slowly, conform and become who someone wants us to be. This is especially prevalent in spiritually minded women, healers and lightworkers who desire to be of service to people. Then one day we wake up and wonder who we are. We're dissatisfied with the status quo, in jobs that are unfulfilling, and find ourselves just going through the motions.   We begin to look for the meaning to life.

During this time, many women turn to entrepreneurship to find the freedom they desire. When we finally step out and start our business our message can be diluted because we are still trying to fit in and be acceptable to family, friends or society. Other times we don't' know exactly what we want but we have a deep inner knowing that we are meant to have our own business. This sets us up for years of dabbling in business. When we embrace the Divine Feminine we are able to heal our voice, speak our truth, so we can own our message and unleash the woman within. Being authentic allows us to stand in our power and create Soul Centered businesses that we desire.

Balance

Balance is necessary for women in all areas of life, not just in business. When we push or force to make things happen or to make money, we fall back into the masculine energies. Women can easily become depleted when they are living in masculine energy and become out of balance in their lives.

Ways we can maintain balance:

o   Listen to the body and honor the cycles of nature to live in balance.

o   Flowing with the day instead of setting rigid

rules.

o Taking time to honor the body and allow for rest and leisure.

o Spending time with other women in community.

o Eating nutritious food to support the body. Allowing time in the day for good self-care. Avoiding long work days and allowing time for life.

o Spending time in ritual to create sacred space for our business.

Creativity

Women are natural creators, it's our spark of life. By exploring our creative ability, we naturally tap into the collective power of creation. In both life and business women need to express their creativity. Creativity is held within our sacral chakra. Our sacral chakra is also where we hold our sensuality. To be fully creative we must also honor our sensual or sexual nature. You've heard the old masculine saying, "happy wife, happy life." This is true. When women have their sensual needs met, we are happier and much more creative. Spending time each week in creative activities, related or unrelated to our businesses keep the creativity flowing. The same goes with our sensual lives. To keep our creativity flowing, we must nurture our sensuality. Creativity and sensuality is what keeps a feminine business flourishing and prosperous.

Collaboration

Sisterhood! For centuries women have come together to strengthen the power of the Divine Feminine and heal others. Together women have incredible power to create change and bring balance to the business world that is out of balance. When women come together in a circle or sisterhood, share their wisdom, and support one another, magic happens. Women meeting with a purpose create powerful ideas, support and community.

One of the ways we can collaborate with like-minded women is through a business mastermind. I now refer to masterminds as a Sisterhood. Sisterhood is one of my favorite ways to network and gain support. In the past 4 years, I have been involved with 3 different sisterhoods. Each one has served a specific purpose. One was to help develop a business model, one was for personal & spiritual growth, and one was a big disappointment but led me to create some wonderful connections with other women. I was meant to be in each one.

When looking for a sisterhood, it's important to be clear on what you need from a mastermind, get clear on your goal, and interview the leader of the mastermind. Take time to make your decision. Watch the methods of the business mastermind leader to see if what the teach and how they operate in business is in alignment with your ways and philosophies. Take time to feel into your decision and the energy of the sisterhood and most of all, follow your intuition.

Masterminds, or Sisterhoods as I like to refer to them, are powerful personal and business growth opportunities. Women give wise council when they feel safe to share their views. Women look at life and business different than men so as a woman, you will gain more from collaboration with other women.

"In the circle, we are all equal. There is no one in front of you and there's nobody behind you. No one is above you; no one is below you. The circle is sacred because it is designed to create unity."
~ Lakota Wisdom

Owning your feminine essence creates an abundant business and life. Women are meant to save the world through Sisterhood. A group of like-minded, dedicated, spirit led women will spread abundance through the world and create massive change. In the Divine Feminine Magic business, there is no competition, only collaboration to a higher purpose for those we serve. I help women achieve their Divine Feminine Magical Business so they can create an impact in their world. A bigger impact in their health, their life, their business and the world. The world will be saved by the spiritually conscious female entrepreneur who embraces their feminine essence.

Katie Henry

Website: www.startingsmartwellness.com

Facebook: http://www.facebook.com/
katiehenry.startingsmart\

Instagram: @katiehenry.startingsmart

Hi I'm Katie. I am a health coach with a background as a doctor of physical therapy and yoga teacher. I had a THRIVING and successful physical therapy practice but it was killing me... I suffered from many of the illnesses my patients had (all sorts of crazy viruses) and then got completely exhausted and burnt out.

During this time I learned that I can't take care of my patients and heal them if I don't heal myself! So I got healthier, and found "balance" (which doesn't actually exist). Most importantly, I learned how to say NO to people and finally say YES to myself. A good diet and exercise is just a small piece of the "being healthy" puzzle. It's about by saying yes to yourself through lifestyle, self care, and mindset shifts towards fueling your body right and sparking joy to live a thriving healing life.

Now I coach healers, healthcare practitioners and ANYONE who cares for others in how to take care of themselves. We work together so you can learn to say YES to finding your spark and reigniting joy in your life!

Follow Your Intuition

& Show Up Authentically

by Katie Henry

Will people like my style? What do I have to say that is different? What makes me so special? Why would anyone want to listen to me? How the heck do I make myself stand out from everyone else in my industry? How can I find my unique voice?

If you have ever asked yourself any of these questions as you are starting your business, the good news is you are NOT alone.

I was asking myself all these questions and more when I decided to make the shift and have a portion of my business include online coaching. I looked around and saw so many other people doing the same thing, but I figured it can't be that hard, everyone wants to be healthy, feel better and have the life of their dreams. I was sure clients will be head over heels to work with me... yeah right?!?

My throat tightened, it became harder to breath and the panic started. It felt like there was an elephant stepping on my chest... How am I going to do this and figure it all out by myself? I felt like a little girl hiding alone in fear in the corner of a dark, moist, bone chilling, shivering cold room. I know the facts:

I am knowledgeable about numerous aspects of health, passionate, giving, and love connecting with others but where do I begin?

I wasn't sleeping, I was anxious and felt paralyzed... then I said to myself, Wait a second isn't this the whole reason why I started my health coaching business in the first place? I became an entrepreneur so that I could heal myself, share my story and help my clients make simple shifts that when compounded created a life full of joy and vibrant health. The panicked feeling stopped but I still felt paralyzed.

And then BOOM...it hit me. I am going to share with you some mind blowing realizations I had. The really funny thing is that they are actually very simple things you just need to remind yourself of.

Mind Blowing Realization Number 1: Just be Yourself

I just needed to be myself. I was stuck in analysis paralysis and comparing myself with other people. When in reality what set me apart was that I was ME! I wanted to share MY story and how I could help people. What was the best way to do that? Being my authentic self. I decided to be transparent and show all aspects of myself (the good, bad, ugly and everything in between).

Once I stopped worrying about what everyone else said I "should" do, I felt a giant weight lifted off my shoulders. That damn elephant moved it's foot off my chest and I could finally catch my breath. Don't get me wrong, I still feel paralyzed at times; however, I'm able to recognize when I shift to this mindset and I tell myself....pump the breaks on these crazy thoughts and just be yourself.

Yes, sometimes I can be a weirdo and goofy but hey! That's what makes me unique! The best part is the more vulnerable, transparent and open I am, the more people want to work with me. I'm not perfect and I show this to my clients. They've told me that this gives them a sense of relief and alleviates their strives for perfection. They know it is ok to slip up and not be perfect....I know I am not perfect and I remind my clients of this daily buy simply being myself.

Not only is this something I am all about in my business, but also in my life. The more you show up as yourself in your business, your relationships and your life, the more you are living an authentic and genuine life.

STOP READING RIGHT NOW! Grab a pen and write down at least 3 unique statements about yourself and embrace your inner weirdo. Don't forget to smile while you do this because you are AMAZING!

Take as much time as needed and really think because this is important.

You should be feeling pretty great right now. I personally suggest keeping that list somewhere handy. I am a huge fan of sticky notes for this list. Sticky notes can be on the wall by your desk, taped on your computer, or taped onto the bathroom mirror. Bust out your list and read it anytime you need to hear that because we all have those doubts creep in.

Break through the fear and stand in your truth, own your story and your business. Just start, don't let fear paralyze you. Believe in your own ability to change lives and notice those voices that are negative, witness them, then reframe it and make positive statements that are true to you and your message.

What is the best part of showing up as your unique self? The more I show up as myself and speak from my heart, the more people respond. It has felt almost magnetic and the clients began showing up out of nowhere. But really, they were silently watching and listening to what I had to say and when I said something they could relate to....BOOM they reached out. Initially it seemed crazy that the more I was myself the more people were drawn to me, but isn't that what the Law of Attraction is all about. Like attracts like. The law of attraction really is true. I raised my vibration and showed up authentically (the good, the bad and the ugly) and amazing people started coming into my life as friends, clients and acquaintances and incredible opportunities and circumstances arose.

In fact, writing this chapter in this book was exactly one of said opportunities.

I realized that my ideal client was really myself just a few steps behind me.

Mind Blowing Realization Number 2:
My clients want to work with ME...not my products, services or packages but ME.

I cannot even tell you how much time I spent perfecting a product or simply writing a newsletter when I started. My newsletters would take me hours to write, add perfect quotes, gorgeous images and elaborate recipes. It seemed brilliant but in reality it was copious amounts of work for little content. Once I realized I just had to be myself, I cranked out newsletters in 15-20 minutes AND more people opened them, responded to my questions and even said things like... Katie I love how authentic you are and I love how to just tell it like it is and speak from your heart. Then, I really feel like I know you and am comfortable asking questions.

Wow my mind was blown. All I had to do was be myself. I got clients based on how I responded to people's Facebook posts. Actually, I have gotten more clients this way than from any advertisements or marketing I have done. The cheapest and smartest thing you can do for yourself and your business is just be yourself. Notice a theme here?

So why not show up as yourself and be transparent, real, and open? Why not, because it can be terrifying to be that vulnerable! BUT if we are paralyzed by fear, we will never grow and evolve. Sometimes (let's be honest... most of the time) the situations that scare us the most are the exact experiences we need to say yes to!

Own your awesomeness. You have a gift to share so open your mouth, grab a pen or start typing and get your message out into the world.

To be honest with you (here is me being open and vulnerable), I didn't think I would be picked to write this chapter. BUT that thinking lasted about 30 seconds because I knew I have nothing to lose and people need to hear what I have to say. What did I do? I went for it because there was something deep inside me that said you have to share your message and your story with other entrepreneurs. I am a passionate person and I'm all about authenticity. When I spoke with the woman organizing this book about what I wanted to discuss, following your intuition and showing up authentically in your business, she said OH MY GOSH we NEED this in the book. Giant sigh of relief! Yes, I knew people would want to hear what I had to say. This brings me to my next realization... trust your gut

Mind Blowing Realization Number 3:
Trust your gut! The right things will happen at the exact right times. Everything really does happen for a reason.

When people say trust your gut feeling, I never completely understood what it meant until I felt it in my body. Words don't do justice to this feeling. It went something like this:

I couldn't pinpoint it but I knew I had to shift. It wasn't just an internal voice telling me to go for it. There was this deep internal burning inside me like a fire had been ignited and there was no way it would be extinguished. I needed to let it out. There was a bellowing right underneath my stomach, a warmth that spread from the inside out, my heart started racing with excitement and my body just wanted to move and dance. I realized that fire ignited deep inside me was my passion for healing others but it wasn't in the way I was serving others only as a physical therapist. I couldn't put it into words but my body told me that I needed to do more, reach more people and shift into my coaching role.

If there is something deep inside you that you can't quite express but need to share you know exactly what I mean. This gut feeling will materialize differently for people. For some it is a surge of energy that tingles your body, others get a crystal clear image or movie of what to do, others have this deep pain in their stomach that doesn't go away until you act on it and some people have their breath taken away. That is why it is so important to slow down and notice how you are feeling because these gut moments or ideas sometimes happen and we ignore them. What we need to do is just go for it without overthinking it. Trust your gut feeling, got for it and don't be afraid to divulge, let it out and get your voice out in the world. Speak up and share your message because there are likely at least tens of thousands or millions of other people who will resonate with your message and need to know they are NOT alone.

Mind Blowing Realization Number 4:
Work hard, always do your best and then have some faith.

Trust and belief that results will come when you do your best.

I embraced my weirdness, my passion and energy for life. I continue to be my authentic self and amazing people and opportunities are coming out of the wood works. But at the same time, I have had to separate myself from people I don't resonate with (super negative people) and that's really hard especially when it's people you have known for years. I have also let go of judgment and knowing that not everyone is going to like me. As a former people pleaser, (but let's be honest - I still have it in me), it is really hard to not be affected by others opinions. But I have to keep being authentic and doing what feels right to me. I am putting trust in the universe and having faith that everything will work out....oh yeah and keep working my ass off!

I had the working hard part down and always doing your best...that's just how I was raised. Fortuitous effort and always going above and beyond is embedded in my being. BUT having faith and relinquishing control to a higher power/ being (God, Buddha, universe whoever or whatever you believe in) was very hard for me at first. Being raised in a strong Irish Catholic family and attending a Catholic grade school and high school and then a Jesuit university, I had a faith and knew the facts about God. Yet I didn't really believe everything I had learned about my whole life so I decided to just shut it down, not go to church and just say I can't believe in anything because there is so much "bad in the world how can there be a God." You know, the typical I know everything 20-something right?!?

I had a shift in my career as a physical therapist, rocky parts in a relationship but still felt like something was missing so I was drawn to deepen my yoga practice and do a teacher training that involved meditation. I learned the value of meditation, slowing down and letting go but also I learned to have some faith and trust. But this wasn't solidified until I had another life shift in my business and a long-term relationship ended. I was back to the paralyzed girl shuttering in a corner out of fear of being alone and rejected. I had a deeper spiritual awakening and realized these major shifts...more like earthquakes... were occurring in my life for a reason. I said it first but then I believed it, prayed on it, meditated on it and found my reconnection to God through prayer, meditation but mostly through human connection. I realized that, yes I can work hard and control many aspects of life but without faith and trust in a higher power, and also in other people, our potential will be limited. When we have faith, trust and know that we are NEVER alone, we are limitless, infinite and impactful. This may have been the biggest lesson I have learned in my coaching business and most importantly - my life. Relinquish control and have faith and miracles truly can happen.

Mind Blowing Realization Number 5:
Get to know yourself deeply.

If we don't know ourselves how can we expect our clients to know us? It circles back to self-care, self-love and self-compassion. When we know and love ourselves, we can show up authentically and speak our truth, which allows us to share our message from the   heart. This is how we can be our authentic self, be present, give generously and connect! When we are ourselves (the good the bad and the ugly), we are more available to let others in and our clients trust us. When they know and trust us, they feel safe and supported. By being myself and giving from a place of gratitude, I have been able to attract those who are more than willing to pay to work with me because they know they are safe, supported and loved. They know that I'll be there to push them and then give them a big hug.

We have to strive for greater, get outside our comfort zone, grow and expand in order to change the world. But if we aren't showing up authentically as our true self, there is no way we can make the impact we know in our hearts we can. So just be yourself, be proud and rock out with your bad self! Be the change you wish to see in the world....take action and BE yourself and your impact will be limitless!

Be your authentic self. I'm a natural giver. I give of my time, talents and skills all the time. People say it doesn't make me the smartest businesswomen. I beg to differ. This is who I am. Giving generously is how I connect with people. If we don't connect with people, how will they get to know us. Connection is what makes us human and a deeper connection with people in general is what I strive for even more than getting a ridiculous amount of clients. I just want to spread my message to the world and I know that the people that end up paying for my services are the exact people I want a deeper connection with. Since I am all about being healthy in a way that works for you and your life and putting yourself first in your life, the more I get to know and connect with my clients the more I am able to help them figure out what will work for them. We are individuals and there is not a cookie cutter recipe for success that is the same for everyone; therefore, we connect with our clients to develop a plan individualized to them and their success. This can be applied to whatever business you do. Understand it's not about you. It's about your client and sharing your heart centered voice.

You might be thinking right now, *Katie, this sounds great and good for you but how the hell do I get to know myself better?* It takes time, but here are a few tricks.

3 Ways to Discover Your True Self and Show Up as You in Your Business:

Take a step back and get away from your busy life.

Learning and understanding yourself is the best thing you can do for your life, your business, your relationships and any human interactions you have. This can be accomplished by taking 5-10 minutes each day to just notice your environment. You can put your phone away on your commute to work and look at others, smile, interact with strangers and just see what affects you in these simple interactions, how you are preserved and how you show up in the world. You can learn a lot about yourself from these simple interactions and you will also be blown away by how a simple smile, hug or thank you can strongly impact another's day.

Sit in silence and take a few deep breaths.

I know this one seems easy but we hold our breaths way more that we realize. You can close your eyes and take 5 deep breaths.... STOP READING and close your eyes and slowly inhale for a count of 4 and exhale for a count of 4 and then repeat this cycle at least 5 times and then open your eyes.

Notice how you feel. You heart rate should have slowed, your thoughts/ worries cleared a little, your body is more relaxed, the tension in your head eases, your shoulders drop away from your ears as you breath a little sigh of relief. Now imagine what can happen if you take more than 5 deep breaths or do this more often OR even sit silently and meditate for 10 to 30 minutes each day. Not only will you learn about yourself but you will learn how to notice the shifts in your body and mind throughout the day, develop more self-awareness and how to relax/destress. These are invaluable skills for yourself and your clients. Yes, slowing down and breathing will take some time and it will take some getting used to but I promise you it will create more time. Why? Your mind will be clearer, your intuition strengthens, and self confidence will begin to flourish. These things all result in a better understanding of ourselves. Remember the better you know and understand yourself, the better you can know and connect with your clients! This is essential to being a successful coach.

Write in a journal and reflect on how you are feeling.

Writing in your journal doesn't have to be specific just write about whatever you are thinking. If you can't think of something to write, just scribble in a notebook, write blah blah blah and the words will come. One of my favorite tricks is to set a timer for 10-15 minutes and just write until the timer goes off and if you can keep writing go for it. Write and reflect daily (even if it is just 5-10 minutes).

As I have been saying, trust your gut, follow your intuition, know yourself and the impact you will make on others. Because when I can be myself and impact another human being and help them reach their highest potential, I am raising the vibration of the good in the world and bringing more joy and more abundance! Even if you work with only one person for several months, you are impacting and improving their lives and starting a ripple effect. If you impact one person's life positively through your coaching, you are slowly but surely changing the world. BUT if you do not do it authentically, what is the point? Authenticity is the cornerstone of a phenomenal coaching practice. Be yourself, be legit and be that remarkable coach. You are exactly who someone needs in their life. You can and will change lives. Get your unique voice out there and go change the world! Be the change you wish to see in the world...what are you waiting for?!?

Melissa Kirkpatrick

Website: http://www.findyourowndrive.com

Facebook: https://www.facebook.com/
FindYourOwnDrive/

Free training:
http://www.findyourowndrive.com/fyod-landing

I'm Melissa, and I own and operate my own businesses which includes our family owned and operated golf course. I am also a health and wellness educator, a self-taught golf instructor, and creator/founder of Find Your Own Drive life coaching for transformation and motivation on and off the golf course.

Married to my high school sweetheart, I'm a grandmother with two adult sons, and a granddaughter. My passion for family and the experiences they share with me brings an abundance of pure joy and fulfillment to my life. As a former high school teacher and as a non-traditional student at the age of 30, I earned my Master's degree in technology education and since learning to play golf in my forties, I now mentor women on the course by offering training and support around the game of golf as well as off the course in the game of life! I believe that how you show up on the golf course is how you show up in life.

As I released my own long time addiction to alcohol, smoking, overeating and spending money, I experienced my own transformation. I have been on the training ground of life and I have the experiences to enlighten and mentor other's to find their own DRIVE. Because that is where the magic begins!

Find Your Drive

by Melissa Kirkpatrick

I recall a time in college, while earning my education degree, I was assigned a project to prepare a presentation for the class that would offer them support as a future educator, in knowing how to motivate their students.

I discovered there were two types of motivation: Intrinsic and Extrinsic.

At that time I didn't even know necessarily what either one of those words meant, but through some research I discovered quickly that we operate mostly from extrinsic motivation - where things outside will motivate us more - such as money, rewards, formal recognition and sometimes to avoid punishment or failure.

Then when I started exploring what intrinsic motivation means, I learned it was a behavior or actions that internally allow for happiness and joy. It's that good feeling that what you are doing is what you like to be doing - a sense of accomplishment and self pride.

This project was powerful for me. From that point forward I realized that I was definitely motivated extrinsically, wanting the gold stars and checkmarks, and to avoid punishment in my younger years to recognition in my adult years.

The ironic part about learning this almost two decades ago is that I have been creating my own understanding of this type of motivation by blending the two together. This is the basis of the process I call Finding Your Own DRIVE.

I believe there is a driving force within all of us. It drives me to get out of bed in the morning, to do the things I need to do, and to show up and be present. We are driven by this internal mechanism that over time is either enhancing our life experiences or sabotaging them.

In order to keep the drive at a higher vibration there is a bit of work that is involved either consciously or unconsciously. To continue making those big decisions and doing those things we have a deep desire and passion to achieve the inner work is through our self talk, visualizations, and beliefs we have created.

For example: When I entered college at the age of 30 raising two children, working full time and having a marriage and home to manage, I recognized that I had an intrinsic motivation driving me to earn my degree to be a high school educator.

My drive to continue working hard and achieving my teaching degree in four years came from knowing that time was of the essence. I wanted to get into my teaching career as soon as possible. I knew the benefits for me and my family which includes being off in the summer with my sons and being more supportive in their developmental years; not to mention the benefits and retirement that comes with having a career in the field of education.

But what really kept me driven every day was this: I could visualize myself being in front of the teenagers I was going to be coming in contact with. I saw myself educating them, supporting them, and offering guidance on their educational path. I was excited to not only to teach the content of the course but to also offer life skills and share my experiences to enhance their learning as well.

So it definitely helped to utilize my visualization. Every day I would think of a different experience that I had while I was in school and how the teachers that I knew made an impact on my life. I would hold onto that feeling while I was creating this new career path for me because that's what lit me up inside.

And four years later I was hired and entered my first classroom as an educator. My desire and vision was now before me.

Fast forward four years into my teaching career, my family became owners of a golf course. I continued to work at the school but also worked part time at the course and managed all the finances.

A few years later we purchased a second course. When this happened, I realized that I was needed more at the golf course full time. So I stepped out of teaching to start working full time   at golf courses. Leaving my career as a teacher so early seemed ludicrous to many, but I knew it was in the best interest for our business and family.

Others had their opinions about me giving up my teaching career after only being in the classroom for seven years and taking four years prior to earn my degree. I heard a lot of reasons why I shouldn't give up my teaching but I knew deep within my desire to be fully engaged in the work at the golf course was far greater than even I could imagine.

I knew something big was there for me and it needed all of my attention!

When I stepped into this active role of being a golf course owner, operator, general manager, finance director, along with hiring and training our personnel, I recognized that there had to be a way to keep my drive.

Unfortunately, I started to go numb and unconscious to my responsibilities by using alcohol, smoking, overeating and spending money. I'm not proud of these addictions and knew they were not serving me. Over time I recognized I had lost my drive and my vision for being on this career path.

I was allowing my ego to take over with the talk of... who do you think you are, you can't possibility be a successful golf course owner. When that doubt took hold I began to mask my feelings with those addictions just to hide out from the chaos and fear that was consuming me.

What occurred to me was this: I lost my drive in receiving any form of extrinsic and intrinsic motivation because of fear.

A few years into living like this, I was confronted and called out on my behavior and actions to a degree that I may die if I don't do something differently. This was my wakeup call and it changed the trajectory of my business and life. I began to recall how my desire to earn my teaching degree came when I tapped into the intrinsic motivation for defying all odds to complete the program. I asked myself, So what needs to change in order for me to tap into that same feeling around the golf courses?

When I went within I heard clearly that three things needed to change and the big one was my alcohol addiction along with taking care of my health and being mindful about my business. So I gave up the addictions and began to focus on me. Self love was new for me to practice but seems to be just what I need most in this transformation.

I asked the big questions of myself:

How can I be happy and joyful as a golf course owner?

What is my intrinsic motivation? What can I do to fully engage in this business?

And what I immediately realized was that I am a woman who owns a golf course and that's pretty damn unique and awesome. In addition, I have the ability to teach!

From this awareness, the first action step was to teach myself how to play the game of golf. I didn't want lessons; I just wanted to experience the game on my own. If I was going to be present in this industry full time, and everybody's going to ask what I shoot and my handicap, I wanted to be able to play and play for my joy and satisfaction. So I learned to play.

Much like I did when starting my coaching practice, I took myself onto the course and just knowing what I knew from observing and working with other people I began to learn. I learned the lingo, etiquette, rules, and how to score. I worked on using different swings, understood the clubs, and spent time on the golf course.

As I evolved into this "golfer", I knew things were different and I had found a new drive!

From this personal experience, I knew this was something other women would want. I began to think, If I can offer them this experience in a non-threatening, non-intimidating way maybe they'll give it a try. Otherwise, if I don't do anything they will miss out on an experience that could be life changing because for me it really was.

Everything was becoming much clearer as to why I am now a golf course owner, and by giving up the addictions I was able to see clearly what needed to happen next. My desire is to give women the opportunity and experience to find their own drive – on and off the golf course.

So deep within me this desire started to evolve and what I recognized first was I'm doing it to make money, I'm doing it so people will pay me, I'm doing this because I want the recognition, all being the extrinsic motivators, but when I let that go and went within the intrinsic motivators showed up.

I am a great teacher and motivator. I have a passion to support women. I know what it's like to reach a certain age or time in your life and feel, Is this it - is there anything more? What else can I do? And I also know how addictions can consume you and take hold and stop the flow of life and dreams. And so I taught myself how to unlock that code of chaos and addiction. This opened me up to the feeling of being aligned to something greater than myself.

Finding my drive motivates me to share and promote this with women. I am allowing them to see themselves fully in their own presence and in learning their own style of play. Teaching them the impact of their language and beliefs on and off the course, praising them for following their desires and passion, and mostly supporting them and giving them a safe place to be open and present to all of their goodness and uncertainties.

By sharing my true authentic self, and allowing my clients to hear and learn about my own good, bad, and ugly experiences and obstacles that I've overcome, they are receiving messages that are now allowing them to make shifts and big changes in their own lives. Being able to witness that and support that is beyond words that can be expressed in this writing.

What I know for sure moving forward is this impact that I am having with my teaching both high school and on the golf course, began back when I was a young girl playing school in my bedroom using my closet door as my chalk board and hanging art work from the ceiling, believing someday I would be teaching and supporting others… and so I am.

I encourage you to tap deep within your internal instincts. I know that for me this motivation for living on purpose, living with joy and ease, being with other women, networking and engaging with them, this is what I've come here to do. This is what drives me. This is what gets me up every day and allows me to show up and be fully present in whatever mental and/or physical state that I might be in. Knowing that these women are receiving from me a gift, a gift that they won't exchange, a gift that they will receive and hopefully pass onto someone else, fills me up with the intrinsic motivation to keep creating and offering more.

But it truly is the drive within. Nothing outside of you is going to be the answer, and when you start from within and do the work and find that drive, that desire, you'll be able to make those big things happen that you only thought you would dream about.

We are all canvases wanting to create new things for ourselves. And we are all mirrors that are seeing what is possible. Aligning your desire with those people, places, and things that can open the opportunity to endless possibilities is all in the asking. Going within, surrendering and asking for what you desire and being open to receive it will allow you to get there much faster. Don't listen to those who are trying to steer your course. You can only know what you want. Be specific, and act as if it has already is.

I knew I'd be a millionaire someday and when I purchased not one but two million dollar plus golf courses with little assets to back the investment and no knowledge about golf, I have arrived at a place where my gifts, talents and experiences would serve others on a playing field much larger than I could have ever imagined.

Where will you take your coaching? No one knows but you! Inside there is a story that only you can write and act out in your life. You are the creator and the seeker of what gives you purpose. When you are open and ready, the gifts you'll leave and the ones you'll receive are all there for you to have an amazing life experience. As a new coach it can be challenging and often times feel like it isn't worth doing the work. When you feel like giving up tap into the intrinsic motivators of why you have this desire to support others.

Now I'd like to share with you my formula for lifting my focus to eliminate any fear or scarcity.
It is to simply start with the DRIVE steps:

D – Desire. What do I desire to have - I want to be a coach and support others.

R – Receive. Take this into your heart space and know that - Being a coach allows me to be in

service to others. And when I'm in service to others I'm being served in return.

I – Implement. Start the action steps on what you can do to allow for this desire to begin to communicate to the Universe you are ready. Start from where you are. Show up in Facebook groups with your message, go to events and network, create a vision board, tell everyone you are a coach who supports others, and most importantly find yourself a coach/mentor that will support YOU.

V – Visualize. See the result you want to happen. Allow yourself to daydream and see how amazing you are as you support and encourage others to grow their life with new experiences. Feel the feelings of what it will be like and see yourself- how you look, what you are wearing, the glow about you. Allow those butterflies to show up and honor them knowing you are reaching beyond your limits to a place of joy, fulfillment, and happiness. Believe those images that appear and show up in your dreams, they are real.

E – Evolve. When you have begun to see things showing up for you and you are offering your services, much like the caterpillar, you will be transforming into that beautiful butterfly; evolving into the person that has passion and purpose for life who has come here to be a witness and support of others.

When the desire begins to waiver on your purpose and moving forward....stop and go within and be guided on what's the best way to take action! What lights you up? Go do those things!

And don't be afraid to ask others. It may be seeking help from someone you just met, asking a question in Facebook, calling a friend, or just going to a networking event. Whatever it takes to come unstuck and ask unapologetically, DO IT.

In addition, for me I have found and enjoy having massages and pedicures when nothing seems to be in alignment. This time for self-care is extremely helpful by allowing for my mind to rest and my body to relax. Often times a small or sometimes large download on what I need to do, have or ask for, will come to mind from this state of being still and open to receive.

And lastly, don't allow your excuses to outweigh your desires! The time is now to Find Your Own DRIVE.

Annika Suoma Frey

Website: www.happyplaceliving.com/happy-list

Facebook: www.facebook.com/HappyPlaceLiving

Twitter: @HappyPlaceLife

My name is Annika Suoma Frey and I am an intuitive happiness coach, helping extraordinary people living extraordinary lives. I live with my husband and my two little boys in the magical South-West of Ireland. My days are filled with love and laughter, making time instead of chasing it, long walks in nature and good, wholesome food. I deeply believe in learning, growing and changing every day, in divine timing, happiness through presence, equality and celebrating diversity. I want to live in a world where we all act and react from love and make conscious choices how we live our lives. I'm sending Love & light your way!

The work that lights me up the most is supporting leaders and creators with the tools I gathered through the many experiences I made. I'm all about bringing ease and flow into your every day life, helping you to breathe again and deal with the overwhelm a life full of transformations brings with it. I love seeing beautiful souls stepping into a new reality when they are leaving old patterns, beliefs and opinions behind them and start loving the body and the life they have while creating an awesome future for themselves.

If you feel that my work is the support you need right now, please feel free to send me an application through my website. I'd love to hear from you and see how I can help you get you to your Happy Place, inside and out!

Everyday Tips & Tricks

by Annika Suoma Frey

I've been coaching people for as long as I can remember. I've coached my mom, my grandma, my sisters, as well as fellow students, colleagues, friends, and my partner. So the first tip I want to give you is one I learned over years and years of doing it wrong.

Never coach without permission.

Why? Because I learned the hard way that when I coached them without permission, I had people walking out of my life. From those I offered coaching to bursting out in tears in public places to a couple almost calling off their engagement after going through a massive transformation with me while I was only there to take their measurements in my seamstress position!

Colleagues in my corporate job who would avoid me after we went into a deeper conversation than they were ready for over lunch one day.

I have a gift and chances are, since you are wanting to learn the basics of being a coach, you have that gift too. I know which question I need to ask to bring into light what is really going on. And I learned that when I ask these questions without having the permission to do so, people get upset. Offended. Hurt. Angry. This happens sometimes because not everyone is willing to look at what is really going on underneath the "I should do this / be like that / stop this behavior / loose weight" noise. But when they are ready and you invite them to have a conversation about the "noise" they will take you up on it. And then you have the permission to coach and work your magic!

Now that we have this very important point out of the way I want to start with the moment you wake up. This chapter is not called Everyday Tips & Tricks for no reason. These are things you can apply and use EVERY SINGLE DAY. And I write CAN very consciously, with the intention that nothing of this has to be done, this is a collection of tools that work for me and you can try them, tweak them and pick out whatever you like and what works for you. We are all different. Our life and our circumstances are different and you know yourself best.

In the morning, when you wake up, what is your first thought? What is the first thing that you do? If it is thinking of all the things you have to do today, reaching for your phone or tablet and immediately checking your emails or social media I urgently recommend you stop that habit. Start your morning with something beautiful, that will set yourself up for a great start into this brand new day.

Many of us have morning rituals. Get up, go to the bathroom, do your body hygiene routine, then eat breakfast. The essentials. Some of us even skip breakfast and get straight to work. I know I did that for many years, denying my body the best start it could have. Now I know better.

But I would ask you to extend your morning routine with something that feeds your mind AND with something that feeds your soul.

As I'm writing this my two children are one and three years old, and most of my mornings look like this:

Waking up by one of them either calling for us, being kicked in the face (the smaller one) or being poked until I lift my blanket so he can slip in (the bigger one). Then, after cuddles and not being able to open my eyes I poke my wonderful supportive partner as long as I need to to get him into a kind of awake state, in which he goes into the bathroom, brushes teeth with the boys and then they go down and have breakfast. Depending on how tired I am I sleep another round, usually until 6:30/7:00am and then get up, do my body hygiene round, get dressed and then I get back into bed.

Yes, you read that right.

I slip straight back in under that warm blanket, turn my meditation on my iPad on and lie there, for 20 minutes, sorting my thoughts, showering my mind. And recently I introduced another piece: 10 minutes of writing, journaling, drawing or writing up a divinely inspired blogpost or offer. Because these come to me in my meditation time and then it feeds my soul to put them right into action. After those 30 minutes, spent clearing your mind, getting still to listen and doing something that lights your soul up you will go into your day refreshed, relaxed and ready.

Now I hear you: I tried meditation before, that isn't for me...maybe yes and maybe no. Yes, these 20 minute meditation and 10 minutes creative practice I do are most likely not what clears and feeds your mind and soul. But there are so many thousands of other ways to do that. And that's the point I want to make.

Find something that wakes you up fully in the morning, not turns just your brain on. We are so much more than just our brain. We are our mind, our body, our soul and if we fully show up every morning just imagine how much brighter, bigger, better our days could be. How extraordinary our life can be. How much better you will be able to serve your clients as a coach by being fully present in your own life and as an extension of that... with them.

Here is a quick list of things you could incorporate into your morning routine, just to get you thinking:
- Go for a short walk

- Do a 20 minute yoga flow
- Read a book for 20 minutes.
- Pray. I'm not religious, but I'm spiritual, so what I mean with this is: pray to whomever you feel is appropriate, the Universe, God, your guides, your guardian angels, your future self...The list is endless.
- Turn music on and dance.
- Breathe. Find a breathing technique that suits you. I love the saying: "Breath is for the soul what voice is for the body."
- Sit in front of a full length mirror naked. Look at you for 10 minutes. Do that for 30 days and you will feel the difference.
- Write a gratitude list.
- Write out ten affirmations, put your hand on your heart and say them out loud, three times each at least, until you believe yourself.
- Set your intention for the day. Every time you feel that you are getting stressed, overwhelmed etc. come back to this intention.
- Play an instrument you love or sing.

I think you get the idea. Do anything that will bring you into a relaxed state, excited for the day in front of you.

If looking at this list got you thinking that you'd like to do ALL these things I have fantastic news: That's my secret plan! But for now pick just two for your morning routine and let's move on to breakfast, or meals in general.

Don't skip meals and make sure that they are as nutritious as possible. Why am I saying this? I lived several years mostly fueled by energy drinks, chocolate and chocolate chip cookies. I can tell you that my energy levels were never lower than in that time. I had so much fog between my mind and the outside world and it brought me to a place where I was overweight, sick and unhappy. I learned this truth in the last 10 years:

Your food is the fuel your body runs on.
The better the food is, the better you show up.

So to make this point short and sweet: Make a conscious choice every single time you eat something. Don't ruin your body by running it on empty calories. It's your fuel. It is the energy source for your body. If you eat consciously you look vibrant and happy and voila, it's much easier to attract clients this way than when you look tired and stressed!

When you are right at the start of your

coaching business you need to learn to set clear boundaries. That looks different for everyone, but here is another piece of the puzzle that helped me tremendously in creating a life and a business I love, every single day. I have an online calendar where clients can book their appointment with me, so I don't have to write back and forth with them. Bonus tip: If you don't have one, get one! There are awesome free ones out there and they even send out automatic confirmation/cancellation/reminder emails.

Every second week I have a look at it and I make sure that the time slots available to book are put around my other priorities and obligations that are important in my life right now, plus that I will have plenty of time to recharge. That includes 15 minutes buffer between calls to go to the toilet, make myself a tea etc.

Which leads me to my next piece of advice:

Put yourself first.
Chances are high that at least one of the reasons you chose to become a coach is to have work life integration and not work around someone else's schedule anymore. So make well sure that you don't trade the freedom you are seeking to accommodate other people again: your clients. Don't offer a time slot whenever it suits them, just open

time slots when it suits you and the life you dream of. Because it starts right here, in this present moment.

A little Truth Bomb for this: The only moment you have any control over is right now. You can't change the past or the future. So start right now with creating a life that you love.

Here is the thing, if they really want to work with you they will make time. If not then they will be frustrating clients to deal with, as the impact your coaching can make on their life will be very limited. And seeing only the limited impact your coaching makes with these clients can bring you easily into a downwards spiral of doubt, worry and fear.

And you don't want to go there. That's not part of the happy, healthy, free life you are dreaming of.

Another thing that can send us down that awful spiral of negative thoughts is hearing "No." to our services over and over again. So here are two more tips that helped me through this and still help me to this day.

1. A NO to your service doesn't mean a NO to you as a person. Most of the time it just means Not right now. If the person took the time to get on a call with you, maybe it was a no pitch

session, a discovery call, a conversation or a Happy Place Session (that's my own process), they are interested in you and what you have to offer. Maybe they are just financially not in a place to work with you right now. They have other things in their life so they can't make the time to work with you. Or, after getting a taste of how intense the work with you would be they got scared and that means they are not ready. YET. But you planted a seed!

2. Make it a game. This is a strategy I picked up in a masterclass with one of the greatest coaches alive, Rich Litvin. Start your own Collecting No's game. Write down everyone you invited to have a session with you. Write down how many sessions/discovery calls you had. And write down how many times you pitched your service at the end and what sum the investment would have been for the client. Do this every single week and I can guarantee you, that after you collected enough No's your first YES will come. It's a numbers game and with every single NO you are winning and are one step closer to the next YES.

The essence is this:

**Instead of taking a NO personally,
CELEBRATE IT.**

The aim is not perfection, but consistency. And if you show up, invite, offer, deliver consistency, every single day, your clients will come. One inspired action every single day will get you much further than doing 20 things one day and then taking out the momentum and not doing anything for a week or two.

Here's another one for you. I learned quickly to make sure that I don't dismiss situations. This was a game changer for me. Now I tell anyone who is interested what I do, no matter if on or offline, family, friends, my hairdresser or the waitress in the cafe. It's like spreading seeds out and trusting that they will grow. Maybe not tomorrow, but they will grow. These people will remember me and my work at some point. It could be that they meet someone and need to tell them about me or they come to a point in their own life at which they are ready to work with me. And then I'm here. And I will be probably a better fit for them then, as I learned even more in the time it took them to come back to me.

I strive to learn and grow every day, to stretch myself. It makes me happy when I learn a new word, technique, skill. I also think it is an essential. You can only help with the tools you have. To be the best coach you could be today, to help others in whatever area it is you do, you need to constantly evolve and deal with your own things along the way. That can happen through a coach for yourself, therapy, reading, learning, expanding. But I deeply believe that if you haven't looked at your shadow sites, your patterns, your beliefs first and are aware of them and working on changing them into the best ones possible, you can't show up and serve fully and completely.

So this is my next tip for you:

While working as a coach helping other people grow keep evolving yourself, keep learning, growing, changing. Live what you teach, as we teach others what we need to learn ourselves the most.

And that brings me back, full circle, to the thing that changed my life, not only as a coach, but also as a mom, a wife, a friend, a daughter. My secret weapon:

The Happy List

Every time I feel like I can't think, whether it's sitting in front of my Mac or iPad trying to come up with a new concept or offer or feeling really exhausted after a client call or meeting... when I feel that I can't think straight anymore I stop and look at my Happy List.

This list has all the items on we talked about earlier in the bit about the morning routine. I learned that if I make time for a little act of self care I get more efficient and overall faster. So a job that would have taken me 2 hours with my mushy brain takes me just one hour if I get up and do 20 minutes of yoga beforehand. That leaves me with 40 minutes where I can do something else.

I just made time by making time for my needs.

I literally just created more time for work when I made time for myself.

So the best tip I can give you is to make your own Happy List, right now. Write all the things down that light you up as a whole: your body, mind and spirit. And then, when you feel your light gets dimmed at any point during your day, pull that list out and   pick one of the points intuitively. Your instinct will tell you what's the perfect thing to do.

If you have a hard time coming up with 10 to 20 points or need inspiration I'd like to invite you to get my example Happy List of 55 items for free here:

www.happyplaceliving.com/happy-list

Kavita Singh

Website: www.earthangelwishes.com

Facebook: www.facebook.com/EarthAngelWishes

Facebook Group:
www.facebook.com/groups/
LoveYourLifeFromTheInsideOut

Instagram: @earthangelwishes

Online Courses:
http://earthangelwishes.teachable.com/courses

Hey Loves! I'm Kavita Singh. I'm an Intuitive Mindset Coach. I love using the Akashic Records, Theta brain techniques and many other shortcut tools in helping women who are at the crossroads of their lives to reconnect with their internal guidance system. This empowers them to stand in their power, bust through their limiting beliefs and take aligned action, creating a life of their dreams!

I've begun my spiritual journey at 16 years old choosing to meditate because I felt called to it. During my 15 years in the corporate IT world, I became a self-help junkie and after many years of immersing myself in tons of books, courses, certified trainings and such I realized that my life experience was the best teacher! We have all we need to be successful in our endeavors in this lifetime. Our breakdowns are actually huge breakthrough opportunities and what we really need is the love and support of each other AND our Divine Guidance System, to treasure and maximize each moment of our journey to living life on our terms!

Intuition and Change

Shifting Our Reality

by Changing our Perspective

by Kavita Singh

I felt icky this morning. My mind immediately came up with the reasons why: "It was because I fell asleep with other people's stuff in my energy. I fell asleep with baggage. In my soul journey via sleep, baggage is not allowed. I wasn't allowed on the train." Train?? I was trying to catch up with the analogy and references that my mind was throwing at me. I tuned into the stream of thoughts again.

"My ego was freaking out yesterday at my calendar today and so the Universe matched it. I didn't do something that was important to my wellbeing." it reasoned.

Huh! I had picked up my phone and stared at it. I was seeing someone's post - FB was the last opened app. And it triggered me. I viewed it as someone being critical of me, rather than viewing it with compassion for the person probably feeling "lonely" because I was suddenly busy and not there for them.

It took me half an hour to shift my frame of mind to

say "whatever this is, I accept it's blessings and surrender it to you, thank you!". I took a moment to breathe deeply and surrendered.

I allowed my mind to shift gears again. I was completely happy yesterday! I was happy, then I saw an opportunity (hint, hint: this one you are holding in your hands right now!) and responded immediately because it resonated with the core of my being. Funny thing about it, my logical mind could not process it. There wasn't any details. I immediately messaged our lovely Kelly (our publisher who posted about the opportunity) and scheduled a chat. And then I let it be.

Yes, that was happiness compounded. I smiled as I read my daily email. It said:

There are really only two conditions of the human experience: very, very happy or about to become very, very happy. Which are you today, Kavita? I'm both. ~ The Universe

I thought to myself, This is hilarious - that I get this message today!

I am being happy for no reason. It was my choice yesterday and it is my choice today. And it will be my choice tomorrow.

If that sounds crazy to you then good! That's the person I love being - happy to tap into the field of unlimited possibilities! This then opens to way for the Universe gives you many reasons to be very, very, very, happy!"

But I wasn't there today. At least not yet.

It took me two and a half hours more to let go of the fact that both of my kids woke up super early. I realized I was feeling... oh I can't get my stuff (my morning prayer/meditation routine) done. Then I thought about my intention to write and today and I realize that today was already unfolding is a perfect example of what to write.

Of course, ask and it is given! I sighed. My Higher Self was waiting for me to get this realization so it quickly chimed in:

What is this situation asking of me?

I leaned into my wiser self to answer:

How about I choose to be present in the moment enough to allow myself to be with my kids. Co-create a moment of joy!

How about changing the priority of my to-do list today to allow another task to get done while I'm in this space?

Consider my affirmations. I say them in-between the things that I do. Oh of course I know this is not ideal mindfulness but it's a space where I can give my borrowed type-A personality something to do when it interrupts my intuitive brain creating zen moments!

And now it has been 3 hrs 15 minutes since I woke up. I recognize a moment of peace - externally. The planes in the sky were no longer present, the distant traffic which occasionally honked held a moment of silence, there was no wind, no pitter-pattering raindrop, no chirping birds...I turned my head to find my toddler, staring silently in awe at the structure of a leaf.

It couldn't have happened if I didn't recognize my need for peace, for silence and owning it in my chaos so that it eventually altered the flow of my reality.

And of course in the recognition of this, I add energy to it and it changes. The hubbub started again as if on cue, but at a hushed tone. This time the energy of it was different. I had already changed my reality and this hubbub moment is incomparable to the last. In this moment, I am stronger, wiser and more peaceful.

My toddler confirms my thinking by crawling into the hammock with me and snuggling her head into the extra folds on my tummy - her favorite spot! She isn't a snuggle bunny in a morning. So I took it as validation from the Universe that I was just where I belong.

I had done a complete circle with the message my Divine Team wanted me to get (or so I thought). We get to choose our thoughts in each moment of our lives. And from this, our thoughts eventually gain momentum and become things. Our power, brilliance and magic all come from the same place. And our mind is that vessel to recognize and translate the thought.

What are you choosing to experience now? How are you choosing to respond to your external environment?

The answer from guidance is also simple:

Be yourself. Choose you!

Of course there are many facets of you - your soul, your personality, etc. It's like having a fully decked closet. You get to choose what to wear, every single day. And your choices creates an interesting life. There IS no right and wrong. All choices exist. So go ahead, CHOOSE your experience!

Today I choose to step into my power. Today I choose to love my life experiences!

I made some mental plans to visit this person and surprise them, however I wasn't able to communicate with them. Today out of all days, I had back-to-back calls and family commitments to attend to. I proceeded to make awesome connections and had the best moments with my older daughter who really needed the extra attention!

Later that evening, I changed my routine. I got home early. I spoke to a friend who give me simplest, most on-point reminder. I paraphrase.... Talk to Archangel Michael. Have him protect you from the energetic punches you get in your stomach when you deal with people who are in their ego mind and their words or emotions are harsh or overwhelming!

Of course! I needed to hear what I already know because now is the time to use it. I did exactly that and faced the music. I was right, the person who earlier had triggered me was lonely BUT deep down inside we always touch on a soul love for each other. Our phone meeting became a beautiful expression of that love. It was absolutely divine! I experienced this wonderful change in reality after I experienced a change in perspective!

Why I'm sharing this? Well because it's just a simple, beautiful reminder to notice whatever is coming up as uncomfortable or ugly in our lives, is really coming up for you to heal it. To choose differently, to shower the issue and its root cause with unconditional love!

And here is the biggest aha for you!

Every big problem doesn't just appear. The Universe always gives us cues on what vibrational frequency we are emitting. That cue was a sign! In this case it triggered me to pay attention! I can keep it or change it if I don't like it, so that it doesn't manifest into irritation, or a full blown sickness to slow me down.

This tiny incident could have been the last straw that broke the camel's back and tipped the scales into something unfavorable. But I shared it as a gentle reminder that we can stand in our power and choose not to experience this downward turn in our energy.

As Lightworkers, we become severely grumpy because the smallest things bother us. Loud noises, not having enough sleep, eating sugary foods, etc. etc. That means an issue that is so relatively insignificant triggers huge emotions that can cause colossal damage to our state of being and how we experience our reality. Yes, it's the responsibility for being on the rapid manifestation lane of life.

If something triggers you, no matter how big or small. Take the time to heal it! Let me rephrase that. Take the time, in-this-moment, and make a decision to heal it now! Today!

I always believe that one of the easiest ways to raise your vibration so that you can leverage the Universe is through gratitude. Gratitude is everything! Give yourself the opportunity to doing this gratitude challenge for 10 days and you will be the one telling me cool stories about the serendipities in your life!

Sign up for your free 10-day Facebook challenge here: http://www.bit.ly/freegratitudechallenge

Misti Patrella

Website: CoachMisti.com

Facebook: The Empowered Entrepreneur
bit.ly/TheEmpoweredEntrepreneur

Twitter: @mistipatrella

My name is Misti Patrella, and I am a Business Coach, empowering women entrepreneurs to step fully into their role as powerful leaders and light bringers in the world.

My business took off when I realized the power of my own gifts and my purpose, and fully embraced them. I have been called to use my gifts to be a part of the upleveling of this planet, and I feel blessed every day to help others be a part of it as well.

From working through limiting beliefs and mindset issues to branding and business strategy, I cover whatever is needed to assist my clients in bringing their gifts to the world through their work, and in abundance.

You Are What You Believe

by Misti Patrella

It took an extra couple of months. For some reason, the first copy hadn't made it. But that didn't matter now, as I was finally opening the protective packaging. This was my sweet proof. It was glorious! A crisp, stamped, very official-looking document was stretched between my fingers. I had been working for 2 years for this moment. And it finally arrived. I had done it.

I had earned the approval of the powers that be, and been granted access to a whole new chapter of my life. I was now a Coach. This certificate had been my next step. I could not wait to go out and start saving the world, one client at a time!

And then…reality set in.

My fingers tightened on the precious ticket to my new career, and the glow started to drain from my face.

Oh, crap. I'm an entrepreneur.

Let me be clear from the start. I was not one of those

natural-born entrepreneurs like my dad, or Gary Vaynerchuk. I didn't have my own business in high school. I quite enjoyed my regular paycheck from my corporate job. And the thought of having to sell anything to anyone made my skin crawl.

Conundrum.

Yes, I was meant to work empowering people to transform themselves.

Yes, I finally felt for the first time because my work was in alignment with whom I was.

And, yes. I couldn't wait to start coaching.

But being a coach in the way that I wanted also meant being in business for myself. That meant I would have to worry about making my own money, and learning how to get regular paying clients. And I did not go into this work to be a sales person. I just wanted to be of service, using my natural gifts and talents.

Good thing for me (and you) that I wanted to do this work so badly. It meant I was willing to at least take a go at being an entrepreneur before I quit. And to make it even more official, I made a commitment to myself.

I gave myself one year to figure out how to be an entrepreneur that could create income in a real way. If after one year, I could see the light towards regular self-sustaining income, I would keep going. If I could not, then I would start thinking of a different plan.

Commitment in hand, I dove right in to the first year of owning my own business.

Your beliefs are the structure of your life. They are what guide and influence the decisions you make. Those beliefs you carry, can either help take you to new heights, or stop you from reaching your dreams.

Getting clear on what you believe about your life, your work, and what is possible for you is essential for entrepreneurs. You want to clearly understand the forces that are driving the decisions you make about your business. And those include your beliefs about money.

Look around you. Take in your surroundings, your life. What does your business look like? How about your income levels? Your relationships? The statuses of all of the things in your life, without exception, are a reflection of what you think is possible for yourself.

I am going to share with you several essential money mindsets that new entrepreneurs must learn to handle. I have definitely bumped into each of these, as have my clients. The best part is that if you can start to work on your money mindset now, it will take you so much farther in your work, so much faster.

Money Mindset #1:

**It is important to understand
what I believe about money.**

Your life is always a reflection of what you believe is possible for yourself.

Whether we like it, or not, our beliefs shape our lives. Henry Ford's well-known quote says it perfectly:

"Whether you think you can, or you think you can't, you are right." ~Henry Ford

Miranda's Magic

Miranda was so excited about the work she was doing as a coach. She had started her business, and was making some money. Her clients seemed to love her. But for some reason, she couldn't make it past a certain point of income. She had visions of making significant income, but for some reason, her actions just weren't paying off.

That's when we met.

After working together for a bit, we discovered the culprit - the real reason why she wasn't making better money. She didn't believe she deserved to. It was a belief that was really holding her back. And she had no idea how much.

Miranda didn't have a college degree. But, she had picked up the belief somewhere in her life that in order to make real money, you had to have gone to college.

Since she didn't go to college, she didn't think a 6-figure income was possible.

This belief affected many things in her business, without her realizing it. She underpriced her services because she didn't think she could ask past a certain amount without the college degree. Once she started to make a certain amount each month, she would unconsciously start to back off of her sales funnel, and book less calls. She had also limited her own vision what was possible for her future, thinking she could only make a certain amount of money in her lifetime. Once she realized the extent to which she was living this belief, she was shocked.

Isn't it interesting how one little belief can affect so many things!?

As soon as we found the belief, we started working on shifting it to something far more empowering. She committed to her self to start taking one tiny shift in action at a time. Miranda started to make more money in her business with very little change what she was doing.

"Whether you think you can, or you think you can't, you are right."

Take time now to get clear where you stand with the energy of money. It will absolutely, and without a doubt affect the entirety of your business.

To find your money blocks:

Take some time to answer the following questions for yourself:

- What are your money habits?
- What is the most you've made in one month in your life?
- What money stories have you picked up from family members or friends?
- What are your personal money beliefs?
- What are you business money beliefs?

Finishing these sentences may also help you to see where your blocks are.

I would be making a lot of money in my business, except_____.

The problem I have making money is _____.

Please note: *It is super important that you do not judge yourself or anyone else while working through the exercise. That only makes the process more difficult for you. Be nice to you, and love yourself through the unearthing of your belief structures.*

When you find a money block:

As soon as you become aware of a belief that may be holding you back, its time to start working to shift it to something more empowering. Simply work on one at a time.

Example: I don't know how to create income.

This belief can be shifted to affirmations such as: I can create real and lasting wealth. Or, I am a powerful steward of money and resources.

Money Mindset #2:
Taking care of my needs creates even more abundance.

When you are working to create something from nothing, like a new business, you need all of your own personal power in order to do it. To get the full strength of your personal power you want all parts of your consciousness and subconscious working together. These are your physical, mental, emotional and spiritual bodies. And they each have their own needs to be met.

> **Physical Needs** – Food, Clothing, Shelter, Enjoyment
> **Emotional Needs** – Harmony, Love, Peace
> **Mental Needs** – Control, Order
> **Spiritual Needs** – Connection to Source/God/ Spirit

Flow vs Stuck

If you are taking care of your physical, mental, emotional & spiritual needs, these four parts work in harmony to help you make incredible things happen. This makes life so much easier, and a whole lot of fun. This is the secret to the mystical state of being known as The Flow.

Being in The Flow makes life such a wonderful adventure, and a whole lot easier. You tend to meet the right people at the right time. Clients come your way with little effort. Ideas pour out of you and are easily created. In this state of being, income flows as well.

If the needs of your whole self are not being taken care of, it creates circumstances that make these parts of you feel unsafe. When things feel unsafe, these other parts of you will start to protect you on their own by shutting down, despite your conscious request for their openness and help. These energies will work against your plans instead of towards them. This begets the unfortunate state of being most often coined as Feeling Stuck.

Feeling stuck leads to all kinds of problems, especially for entrepreneurs. Your actions stop working, which usually means you are not making the money you want. You start attracting clients who are not in alignment with your work. Frustration and irritation sets in, increasing the level of stuckness you feel. Illness can set in here too, forcing you to slow down, and work to get things back in alignment.

What to do when you are feeling stuck:
It is easy to run and ask for assistance during this time. But I would urge you to look inside for answers first, and then approach someone for help if necessary.

It is essential to learn to trust your self as you grow your business. And this is a perfect place to start. Put your hand on your heart, take a couple of deep breaths, and ask your heart what is out of alignment, and in need of support. You will get an answer. When your heart/soul speaks it is usually in a soft voice, so listen well.

Funding Your Adventure
(Don't Quit Your Job Quite Yet!)

I love the entrepreneurial spirit. It attracts people who are so ready to create something different for themselves and the world. Yes! We need more of that.

I also see this spirit of risk get overzealous, at times. Many entrepreneurs come to me and say, "I have the best idea in the world. I've created it in my head, and I've built a website. I've quit my job, and I'm ready to go!" And almost every time, they later regret that decision.

Remember that taking care of your physical needs creates abundance. But the opposite is also true! If you are constantly worried about making money as quickly as possible, it adds so much more stress to you and your business. It creates a fear of messing up. Add in a healthy dose of stress to make as much money as soon as humanly possible. All of this stress just plain takes all the fun out of it. If you don't fix it, you hit the downward spiral of negativity and burnout. And I can pretty much guarantee that you won't be successful from that space. I firmly believe this is one of the biggest reasons so many new businesses fail.

This work takes time. There really is no such thing as an overnight success. It just looks that way from the outside. My research shows that the average coaching business takes 2-3 years to start running on its own. Your path may be shorter, or longer. Regardless of the amount of time, please set yourself up for success, instead of failure. You can do this by keeping your current job for as long as possible, or until your new business starts making enough money that you can afford to quit. Which ever happens second. Then your transition between careers can be much smoother. Ideally it is a major stepping- stone and celebration!

Pay Yourself – First & Always

Would you take a long-term, full-time job where you didn't make any money? Nah, me neither. However, this is exactly what so many coaches do to themselves when they start their own business. And as soon as they make any money, it immediately goes to pay bills, or is invested back in the business.

Get in the habit of paying yourself first. Pay yourself as soon as you receive the income, and before you start sending funds anywhere else. This could be either a percentage of the whole, or a fixed amount every time. What ever works for you. And put it in an account that is for you to spend on the things you really want. When I got started as a coach, sometimes I would pay myself only $5 if that was all I could afford. But I did it every time. This small action creates abundant pathways between you and your business that keeps the energy of money flowing, even if it seems like there isn't a whole lot to go around.

Money Mindset #3:
I clearly understand how to create regular income in my business.

I heard someone say once that coaching isn't a

business. At first I thought, "How dare they!" But if you think about it, it's quite true. Coaching itself isn't a business. It's a skill, a tool. That skill needs to be crafted along with your other skills, gifts and talents into a business. And the very first order of that business must be to figure out your way to create regular income.

I've said it several times because it's so important! Your business needs to pay you back. Otherwise it creates so much unhappiness. So make this priority number one.

There are many, many ways to make money as a coach. You are only limited by your creativity. You may have to try several things. That's okay. And please don't be afraid to mess up. I would list some ways here, in fact, I almost did. But I don't want a silly list in a book to limit you either. Go out on the inter-webs and look around. See what's stirs up your imagination.

If you are having a hard time getting started, time to do some research. Get crystal clear on what your ideal clients want and need from you. I'm sure the list is long. Create a list of 25 things that can help them work through transformation. Look to see what coaches and other entrepreneurs are doing to create income. Another very important consideration to keep in mind: what seems like fun for you? Don't forget, you'll be doing this a lot, so do something that seems exciting and fun for you!

Tasks That Make That Money!
So many entrepreneurs I speak to want to immediately start creating a website, writing their blog and spending

time in social media because that's what they think they are supposed to do. While those are all wonderful tasks, not one of those tasks is directly linked to creating income. Yes, you need a website, but it isn't going to make you money - especially not in the beginning of your business. A blog is a good idea, but not a moneymaker.

Here's the biggest difference between having a corporate job, and being an entrepreneur:

In the corporate world, you get paid to be busy. In the entrepreneurial world, you get paid when you get clients. It's a totally different mentality. It threw me off guard when I started my business. I would work hard all day long. At the end of my day, I was pooped. I had done so much work. Yet hadn't made
$1. That's just not okay.

A good rule of thumb when you are getting started is to spend 2/3 of your time on work that is going to make you money. This helps to keep you focused and get used to a slightly different routine. My tasks linked to creating income are creating and launching new offers, discovery calls with potential clients, writing any content that has an offer attached, writing talks, following up with past and potential clients, and developing new courses. I dare you to come up with 15 more tasks for your own business!

The other 1/3 of your time can be spent on the administrative needs of your business - like your website, blog, videos, or even writing your next book.

As you can see, your money mindset very much influences your business. The bright side is that you have control over your mindset, and can work to shift it to whatever is most powerful for you. I invite you to grab hold of your mindset and look at the creation of your business as a grand experiment and adventure. Enjoy the process!

Carla Gibson DC

Website: http://www.carlagibson.com

Facebook: https://www.facebook.com/
carlagibsondc/

Twitter:@carlagibsondc

LinkedIn: https://www.linkedin.com/in/carlagibson

Carla Gibson, D.C. has a passion for empowering women to live to their highest potential by being completely supported in their own self-care. Trained as a chiropractor at Life University in Marietta, GA, Dr. Carla employs a variety of techniques to bring about a transformation in the health and wellbeing of the client by addressing all levels of the triad for health – mental/ emotional, chemical/bio-chemical and structural. Dr. Carla teaches clients what it takes to be successful in life. Noting the incomplete nature of most health care, Dr. Carla created Triad Health Alliance where she works with clients to develop individualized care plans which create the opportunity to reach goals in every area by bringing integrity to their health.

Services are offered in a traditional office setting and through intensive retreats with online follow-up.

Dr. Carla lives in Tempe, AZ with her family and enjoys spending her free time hiking and deepening her own personal growth and development.

Be Your Ideal Client

Success Starts with Self Care

by Carla Gibson DC

If you've ventured into the world of being a coach, then you've probably been through some personal development of your own. Whether you've spent thousands of dollars on transformational seminars, or you just noticed that people like to talk to you and somehow they leave feeling better for it, you've done something in your life to transform dis-ease into ease and now you're passionate about sharing that with others. My own journey has included availing myself of a variety of healers, attending seminars and engaging in personal development programs. My participation led to a desire to have an impact on the world and I felt strongly   led – by intuition or insanity – to pursue professional training as a chiropractor.

Everything I have learned through my own healing journey has allowed me to contribute to my clients at a higher level. I've learned thousands of ways to be more engaging and more effective as a practitioner, but what I want to share with you is consistently the most valuable tool to my success – be your ideal client. Over my years of inspiring others to their highest potential, I've noticed the frequency, consistency and duration of my own self-care depreciates remarkably when I get "busy" serving others. If I were to graph my sales and effectiveness I would most likely see a direct correlation between the times I was taking steps to inspire and support myself and the times I was having a lasting impact on the most people. And conversely, I would see that when my impact was off the mark, so was my self-care. This illustrates that self-care is not a luxury, but in fact essential to our ability to help others. May the explanation and the exercises provided here be of service to you and in turn, bless those you serve.

Identify your Ideal Client and Find Yourself

The ideal client for Carla Gibson, D.C . and Triad Health Alliance is a woman, age 35-55 who feels stuck in their life even though it seems they have tried EVERYTHING but nothing provides the results they seek. They understand their health and success are their responsibility and they are looking for a skilled guide to navigate the myriad of options and to determine their specific path for healing and growth.

Your ideal client is whomever you have defined to be the client you will spend your time, money and resources attracting. Once you know exactly who you serve and what they need, honing your message and marketing becomes easy. But don't stop at creating sales funnels and lead pages with this information, use it to create your own self-care plan. There may be some differences between you and your ideal client (age, gender, etc.) but from your description of your ideal client, define who YOU are and what you are looking for in the realm of personal development and self-care.

Let's dissect my "ideal client" and look at me as an example. In my description, my ideal client is stuck. Your ideal client may be successful, unsuccessful, suffering, empowered, enlightened, unaware, happy, sad, frustrated, ready, peaceful, frantic, overjoyed, scared, addicted, recovered, seasoned, newbie, etc.

Using your ideal client description, take a minute to identify who YOU are right now in these areas:

Health

Physical_____

Mental_____

Emotional_____

Spiritual_____

Relationships

Family_____

Relatives_____

Intimate_____

Friends_____

Business Associates_____

Community_____

Currency

Money_____
Job_____
Career_____
Finances_____
Time_____
Space_____
Energy_____
Assets_____

In the description of my ideal client, I identify with being STUCK! Today, I would say I'm stuck in the areas of physical and emotional health, intimate relationships and money, space and   time.

How do I know this? Well, let's talk for ten minutes and you'll probably hear me complain about all of these things in one way or another. There may be other areas where I'm happy or seasoned – relationships with my kids and energy, for instance. But my ideal client is STUCK, so I'm going to look at how I nurture my STUCK areas so I can maximize my impact with those people. I might also seek out coaches for other areas, but if it comes to prioritizing my resources and time, I'm always going to get the most out of caring for myself in the way I help my ideal client care for herself.

You may wonder, If I'm still not perfect in an area am I qualified to help others? I've felt that way myself at times. It's important to know that being perfect in the area you coach isn't what makes you a great coach. It's what you DO about your own imperfections, who you're being and what you're willing to share with others about your journey that creates your value as a coach.

Mastery Tip:

Do this exercise every quarter and commit to taking action in an area of your life by doing something different – hire a new coach, say something different about the area, have a conversation with someone, etc. Continually addressing your own areas of growth will continually bring you new opportunities to help others.

Being my own ideal client means that I am seeking a skilled guide to help me in an area where I'm stuck. There have been times in my life as I've made the transition from "stay at home mom" to "practitioner" to "doctor" and "chiropractor" where I've thought, I know all this, what can someone else do for me?

And I will tell you, the months I wallowed in this righteousness were the most painful and financially desolate months of my life. I had a story that I knew it all and I didn't have any extra money so I couldn't get help. I paid for other types of services – business coaching, copywriting, book design, online marketing tips – thinking I needed to develop myself in those areas where I didn't have expertise. In these areas I might have defined myself as "ready," "frantic," and "newbie." I imagined devoting resources to these areas would propel me to success in business. None of it was wasted, but it was ineffective and in some cases, extremely frustrating for both me and the people I hired. Why? I was not taking care of myself in areas where I was stuck – depression over moving, losing a relationship, feeling lonely, physical disease, subluxation and spiritual bankruptcy. Without addressing those areas in the ways I hope my "ideal client " would, I couldn't be effective in anything else.

When you find those areas where your experience matches that of your ideal client, do whatever it takes to invest in the resources needed to support you in THAT area. Resist the urge to spend your resources on more business tools, more training, more marketing and more advertising. Take all that money, time and energy and use it to hire the person you respect the most in your area of expertise and dive into lovingly and completely getting what you need the way you wish your clients would. If you want to be really courageous, take on some type of modality or tool you have a racket about. I did this with Emotional Freedom Technique (EFT). I had tried it many years ago as a patient in Dr. Mercola's office. It was effective, but I couldn't stick with it and I believed it just didn't work as well as other modalities. I had the opportunity to utilize EFT in a course I joined. It was a course on relationships and I joined kicking and screaming at the request of a friend. I didn't have time to work on my relationships because I was busy opening a new practice and trying to spend more time with my kids. How could "Attracting the Love of My Dreams" possibly be important?

Hint: If you're resisting addressing an area, you might be STUCK! As it turned out, shining a light on my "stuck" with EFT made a huge difference and I went on to have the most productive and successful months in my practice. And I met "the love of my dreams" in the course too!

Share Yourself Authentically

What you'll learn quickly as a coach is that people don't always tell you what's really bothering them. They'll do anything to look good and to tell you what they think you need to hear. The best way to create a safe space for people to share exactly what's going on for them is for you to be comfortable with sharing yourself. The most success for me has come during the times I've been willing to share myself authentically. Instead of staying stuck and hiding the fact that I was stuck in some of the very areas I help people with, I began sharing where I was stuck with everyone. Even my clients! Be clear, there is a difference between "sharing authentically" and "dumping" on people. You need to become skilled in sharing yourself in a way that does not make the other person responsible or burdened by what you are sharing. You'll know you are being authentic when the people you are sharing with feel touched, moved or inspired and see something for themselves in what you've shared. If you don't have training in this area, I recommend the Landmark Forum or PAX International to help you learn. Once you're clear and confident you can share yourself authentically, talk to people. Share with them what's working for you and what's not and speculate on why. As you'll see below, sharing yourself is the only way to "close the gap" and it also brings you a sense of peace and belonging that can't be created any other way. If this seems scary, just commit to doing it for a day and see what opens up for you.

Close the Gap

When you serve, the potential to create a gap is real. In my community I was seen as "having it all together." While this provided a source of strength and support for many, it created what I call the Heroine Gap. It was great for my ego to be seen as a somehow ahead of them and it was good for them that I had a knack for organizing resources. I learned later I was also creating a "less than" for them, inadvertently. I learned this one day when I let myself be vulnerable with one of my favorite clients. I told her what I was dealing with in my personal life and she breathed a sigh of relief. I asked her why she reacted that way. She told me, "I didn't think you had any problems and you had it all figured out. It helps to know you're not perfect." I was shocked! Why wouldn't she want me to be perfect? Wasn't she paying me to solve problems for her? Didn't she want to know that I was better than her?

No, it was actually the opposite. When she learned that I struggled and failed just like her, she could listen to my suggestions as sage advice rather than as prescriptions for perfection that she was sure she could never obtain. It changed our whole dynamic and made me a more effective coach for her.

What would it create for you to close the gap and to share yourself authentically in your communities and especially with your clients? Where could you get support for your own journey and get yourself unstuck in a way that provided you with more energy and more resources to share with those you serve? How could being your ideal client – one who admits you need help and reaches out for a trusted guide and commits to making real change in your life – actually increase your reach beyond the next sales funnel or call to action?

Please email me at : gibsonwellness@gmail.com and let me know what you discover for yourself by going through the inventory above and being willing to invest in yourself at the same level you expect of your clients. I welcome your feedback and the opportunity to celebrate your success with you!

Patti O'Leary

Facebook: www.facebook.com/PattiOLearyCCM

Email: ChoiceswithPurpose@gmail.com

My name is Patti OLeary. I am an educator, certified Nutritional Therapist, and Integrative Health & Life coach. I am on a mission to teach women how to create clarity and take small sustainable steps toward living healthier, more empowered lives by making Choices with Purpose.

I have lived in Massachusetts and New Hampshire most of my life, and relocated to Nashville, TN six years ago. But I am NOT a Yankee…I am a Red Sox Fan! As a matter of fact both of my amazing children, Andrew & Casey, have worked for the Boston Red Sox!

I have a gift for teaching and it is an absolute passion of mine, with over 12 years experience in special education, teaching and supporting a variety of learners of all ages. I love helping you discover how you learn best, while providing tools and support that connect information in a way that not only makes sense but can easily be applied. It is my desire that everyone become life long learners.

When I am not teaching and coaching, I can be found (day or night) out on the lake bass fishing with the love of my life, Chuck.

Team Management?

"Teamwork makes the dream work." ~John Maxwell

by Patti O'Leary

As a new or beginner coach you may be thinking, I would love to manage a team, but I really don't see having that on my to do list for a while yet. I need to get paying clients first.

What if I told you the two were connected?

As a coach and an educator, I am here to tell you even if you do not have a team to work with yet, working to build your skill set in Team Management is a must do for any coach, even beginners. You wouldn't expect someone who is an expert in crisis management to wait until a crisis to learn crisis management would you?

No.

The same is true for learning Team Management, you need to learn the skills before you can apply them. Good team building and management skills are important to your coaching success.

Let's explore why this is true.

One of the most important aspects of Team management, or classroom management for that

146

matter, is not only about how well we can manage a team, it is primarily about how well we can manage ourselves! As Team Leaders we must know how we communicate best and what character strengths we have firmly in place and identify which character strengths need a little more exercise.

If this seems overwhelming, no worries, I have a few tools to share with you that I find invaluable. These tools will not only help you develop a better understanding of yourself, but they will also help the people you serve, and the team members you will eventually surround yourself with.

One of the first tools I use is the VIA Character Strengths Assessment, specifically for the coach and coach/client team management model. https://www.viacharacter.org/

What benefit do we get from knowing our Core Character Strengths?

Knowing our core character strengths isn't just interesting information. Character strengths can actually have a significant positive impact on our lives.

Research shows that by understanding and using our character strengths we can:

- *Strengthen verbal communication and listening skills*

- *Better manage and overcome problems*
- *Improve relationships*
- *Enhance health and overall well-being*

The self-assessment takes less than 15 minutes and provides information to help better understand how core character strengths align. This assessment is very positive and focuses on your best qualities. Once you complete the assessment, you will be able to read your results and download a free printable copy!

There is even an option for coaches to set up a VIA Pro Site, which provides a unique survey link to send clients allowing them to take the free VIA Character Strengths assessment.

When a client completes the assessment they will be provided a beautiful downloadable version of the results as well and you will be sent an email notification. The client results will be accessible to you under your "Clients" tab. (You can see mine in the appendix of this book!)

I usually download a copy of the report to review with the client at our first session.

A great simple way to use the VIA Character Strength Assessment report in a coaching session is to highlight the Key Concepts of the top two strengths, you can learn more about these by clicking on the character strengths tab at the top and each strength has a short explanation you can use as a guide.

Next, I discuss the bottom three strengths with the client. I often state the key concepts and share information on exercises for boosting that strength.

What I love about this assessment is how positive it is. Everyone has the same 24 Character strengths in varying degrees and the assessment is designed to show how those strengths align and determine a unique profile for each person.

There is a wealth of understanding and knowledge gathered to help guide coaches and clients to the best version of themselves.

You can also take advantage of the amazing training programs VIA offers coaches.

Now, let's get an idea of what a team looks like in coaching.

The definition of a team is a group of people who depend upon one another to accomplish a specific set of goals. The team has a shared interest in the outcomes of these goals, and members are viewed as one unit.

Another point to remember is that although teams are made up of groups of people, not all groups of people are teams.

What are some of the models in coaching where you can use Team Management Skills? There are several Team management models in coaching:

- *Coach/Client*
- *Coach/Group*
- *Coach/Support staff*
- *Coach/Other Coaches (Peers).*

What are some basic components of an effective team?

There are many, but I want to address what I call my top seven: Purpose, Participation, Communication, Strengths, Group Dynamics, Agreement, and Overall Team Effectiveness.

Purpose: Members of the team have to know why the team was formed in the first place. Team members will work together for one specific goal. Teams help solve specific problems and maintain a common focus.

Think about it: What is your team's purpose? This is crucial information!

Participation: Team members are often selected based on their skill set or expertise. Team members are more effective when they feel they have something to contribute rather than when they feel obligated. Encourage participation by recognizing value.

Think about it: How will you recognize team members' contributions?

Communication: This is a key component. In today's age access to team members is usually not a problem. We have cell phones, internet, Skype, webinars, teleconferences, so many options, but truly effective team members must agree on how often they will communicate with one another and what method they will use to communicate. It is normal to challenge others' ideas but be respectful at the same time.

Think about it: What strategies will your team practice to ensure they are communicating effectively at all times?

Strengths: Team members are gathered not only for their skills but also on how one member's skills will work with another and how those skills will compliment those of the rest of the team.

Think about it: How will each team members' skills work with and compliment other members' skills?

Group Dynamics: Small teams often interact, communicate and share information quickly and easily; they stay motivated and understand the importance of each member's contribution to the overall team.

Large teams also have advantages. Large groups

are able to split up the work more easily and have experience, skills, knowledge and resources to accomplish goals faster. As a team leader, you must be mindful that large groups can begin to fall apart when communication breaks down.

Think about it: How will you facilitate effective communication and focus within the team regardless of its size?

Agreement: Team members must agree on group rules, roles and norms. Who will be the timekeeper? Who will be the note taker? Who is the team meeting facilitator? Are cell phones allowed to remain on during team meetings? Establish rules, roles, and norms upfront. Be consistent.

Think about it: How will you monitor and ensure the team agreement is consistently met?

Overall Team Effectiveness:
A team's effectiveness is measured by its performance, outcomes and attitudes. By having clear goals that can be measured and monitored you will help ensure the team will successfully reach their goals and that the process for reaching those goals can be duplicated again and again.

Think about it: What processes will you create to maintain effectiveness and will that process be duplicable?

A great assessment resource I use when consulting and training about Team Management is the Tony Robbins DISC Profile, available FREE for you here: https://www.tonyrobbins.com/ue/

The Tony Robbins DISC Profile is a 15 minute online assessment based on the theory of behavioral dimensions. The research behind this assessment revealed four main quadrants of behavior and personal preferences: Decisive (D) How you tend to approach problems and make decisions, Interactive (I) How you tend to interact with others and share opinions, Stabilizing (S) How you tend to pace things in your environment, Cautious (C) Your preference for established protocol/standards. By completing the Tony Robbins DISC profile you will have a better understanding of your behavioral style and how you present yourself and interact with the world around you.

There are many other DISC assessments available online that you, as a coach, can have access to. I prefer the Tony Robbins DISC profile for several reasons:

- It is FREE!
- The assessment is not overly language based like many other DISC assessments, which can be confusing for some because of the wording used in the questions. Other DISC assessments can be manipulated to reveal a desired quality or trait, instead, the

Tony Robbins DISC Profile lessens the ability to manipulate the results by asking you to rearrange words and phrases by dragging them and placing them in order of preference from MOST like you to LEAST like you.

- The results are presented in two, outstanding, multipage reports, a Personal Strength Profile and a Values Index Profile that completely outline your unique skills and behaviors.

I usually have the business groups I am consulting for complete the assessment based on how they are at work. I have my coaching clients complete the assessment based on how they are at home. Yes, by setting that mindset criteria for completing the assessment beforehand you will produce very different results.

The first report, called The DISC profile, is very comprehensive and reveals how the person behaves in a natural state vs. an adaptive state.

A natural state is described as how a person behaves when they are being their least stressed, their most authentic and natural, it is their basic style, their true self. When a team member is in this state they are working at maximum efficiency and productivity.

An adaptive state is how a person behaves when they feel like they are being watched or closely monitored and micro managed. If a team member stays in an adaptive state too long they become highly stressed and less productive.

I really like the data gathered through this particular assessment because several areas are identified that are key to understanding your team members' strengths:

- *Behavioral Strengths*
- *Communication Style*
- *Ideal Work Environment*
- *Effectiveness by understanding behavior*
- *Behavioral Motivations*
- *Continual Improvement Areas*
- *Preferred Training & Learning Styles*

With the results from the Tony Robbins DISC report, a team manager has a 'secret decoder ring' that helps develop a clearer outline of how to optimize the effectiveness and productivity of each team member.

The Values report results, calculated from the data gathered in the original assessment, are a combination of the research into what drives and motivates people, how they use their talents, and how to maximize performance and passion.

In Team management it is important to know what motivates your team and how to use those motivations effectively.

The Values report provides this information by measuring dimensions of motivation in a   person such as a drive for balance, economic return, uniqueness, influence, helping others, establishing order, and a drive for knowledge. This knowledge of a person's motivation is like having the Golden Key to goal setting and goal reaching success!

Bonus! At the end of both the DISC and the Values reports are a series of reflective questions for the team member to complete on their own. Answering these questions helps to facilitate the learning provided by the reports in a way that not only connects the learning; it allows the team member to better understand their motivation, values, and strengths which in turn empowers them to become more powerful assets to themselves and the team.

Now, are you beginning to see how valuable this tool can be when working with clients too?

Will you make a good team manager?

Of course you will! You are already taking the time to learn what team management is and how it will not only benefit you as a team leader, but as a coach too.

There are a few more hallmarks of a great team leader to keep in mind:

- **A great team leader effectively communicates expectations with clear goals.**
- **A great team leader is thrilled when team members achieve success and expresses**

appreciation for the effort.

- **A great team leader empowers people with honesty and transparency not hidden agendas.**
- **A great team leader inspires others to keep reaching, learning and growing.**

Congratulations!

Look what a great leader and coach you are already becoming, with a new appreciation and understanding of what Team Management is and your role in it

By using the tools suggested, and continuing to learn and grow as a leader and a coach you are destined to lead very successful teams of clients, groups, support staff, and peers.

A story for you...

Recently, I reached out to another coach who has been trying to grow her business; she had a particular skill I didn't and I suggested that we would be a great team to work together. She wrote back:

"I've been told that I'm not a team player, and it's true. Please don't be offended, but in all honesty I work better as a solo act."

OUCH!

It stung at first to hear that. Little did she know the

working together I was suggesting was going to benefit her, not me, because I already had clients who were in need of her services. So, not being a team player cost her an opportunity to grow her business reach.

Learning about teamwork management can open up opportunities. Team Management is more than becoming a team leader; it also includes learning how to become a better team player.

"Coming together is the beginning. Keeping together is progress. Working together is success." ~Henry Ford

Aliza Bloom Robinson

Website: www.alizabloom.com

Facebook: http://www.bit.ly/findingease

Twitter: @alizabloom

LinkedIn: https://www.linkedin.com/in/aliza-bloom-robinson-58970b24

Aliza Bloom Robinson is committed to touching hearts, freeing souls and transforming lives. She is a master spiritual coach and facilitator, author, speaker and ordained Unity Minister. Founder of Divine-Awakening.org, Aliza's presence will touch your heart and inspire your own journey. Aliza guides you to discover fulfillment and your greatest potential, freeing you to live the life you've always longed for. She facilitates the discovery of peace, purpose, passion and clarity. Aliza brings a sense of fun, delight and ease to all she offers.

Aliza's first book, Be a BOA, Not a Constrictor, available in the Kindle store, is an inspired fable for authentic transformation, becoming BOA; Bold, Outrageous, Authentic. She also is a contributing author in the Best Selling 365 Series, 365 Ways to Connect with Your Soul and 365 Moments of Grace. Her most recent Amazon Bestseller is Falling into Ease: Release Your Struggle and

Create a Life You Love is available as a paperback and ebook everywhere fine books are sold.

To get to know and experience Aliza more, she is offering exclusive membership in her private group "Finding Ease". You can join her here:

http://www.bit.ly/findingease

Saving Your Soul

While Giving Your All

by Aliza Bloom Robinson

You are a coach, you love your work, you know you have a gift. In the beginning you were all excited to dive in, to work with as many people as you could, to make a difference and an abundant income. It's all going along pretty well until one day, you notice, it's not quite as easy to get up in the morning, you are exhausted at the end of the day and there is still more to do, or the income just isn't flowing like you thought it would. What happened?

If you are a coach, especially a newer coach, it is easy to over give, to work harder than your clients and to stay so busy that you forget your needs. Don't do that! I call this losing your soul; I use it loosely and with a playful lightness.

Typically, and I'm not saying that you are typical, we as coaches, get into our businesses with the desire to give, the desire to make a difference in the lives of our clients. Some of us get into the business because we are tired of the corporate or "job" lifestyle and want to be entrepreneurs. Others because it is a deep soul calling; one that you can no longer ignore. It looks like a dream career from the outside and often is. However, it is not usually a simple straight forward path to success, it's more like a windy road with tons of opportunities to heal your own wounds and truly step into the brilliance that you are here to be.

The journey to soul success involves and includes the healing of our Souls. When we take a stand for ourselves, when we uplevel our life experience, there are things that need to go. Things to be released or healed.

The deeper I've gone into bringing my most authentic self to the world, the deeper the wounds I've gotten to heal. We are here to be light workers, we are here to discover our Essence and that Essence is free of wounding and separation.

On the journey of entrepreneurship, there are many opportunities to heal, to stretch and to grow. Many of us believe that we can simply get clients and make a good income, but if you are truly called to this work it becomes a whole journey of body, mind and spirit.

I am a spiritual coach, facilitator and vibrational catalyst, but prior to this I was an ordained Unity Minister for over 16 years. Both careers began as a calling and an upleveling that involved deep soul searching, release of the old and a stepping blindly into the new.

When I left church ministry, I found myself on a spiritual pilgrimage that lasted several years. I thought, Oh this will be an easy transition because I've been coaching spiritually for years.

But what I was being called to was so much more, it required my entire soul to come into alignment. So I dove deep.

We as coaches, especially the women like to give. And over give. And give some more. We can see so clearly what our clients should or could be doing to improve their lives and we want to help! We know we can do good and we will give everything we have to help.

That's a good thing, right? Let's look at that last statement again. We will give everything we have to help. What is your response to that statement? What is your reaction to it? Just notice. Everything! Yes or No? Become curious.

While we are givers, it does not serve us well to over-give.

Listen up here. Do not over-give!

I'm not saying don't give your all. I am saying don't give over your capacity in any moment. If we aren't careful we will give so much of ourselves away that we have nothing else to give. When this happens we risk being dried up, burned out and eventually become no good to anyone else.

I am a spiritual coach and the soul work is my specialty, but prior to being a coach, I was an ordained Unity Minister for over 16 years. In both careers, I had to learn to take care of myself, my heart and my soul first and foremost.

The first time I burned out, it caught me by surprise. I didn't see it coming and it knocked me flat. The problem wasn't that it kicked my butt, but that I still didn't take care of me. Instead I gave more, and more, and more. Somehow I thought that just a little more would make all the difference in the world and everything would turn out alright again.

I was wrong! Once we hit burnout, there is a journey back to wholeness. I want to prevent that in others!

In coaching, as in ministry, there are a zillion ways (ok, maybe not quite a zillion, but the ways do come out of the woodwork, if you aren't conscious) to be distracted. Ways to put your own soul last on the list. There are people who think you are super human and don't have a life outside of them. There is the behind the scenes work of marketing and social media, planning and technology. There are those who expect you to give endlessly and without boundaries. There are those who have no personal boundaries and want you at their beck and call, every moment, every day.

In ministry, as in coaching, self-care is essential. On the physical realm, it is essential to eat well, to move our bodies with exercise and to rest – to take breaks from work and to sleep well at night.

Those are basic physical needs. But what about the Soul needs? Soul-care is as necessary as self-care. The soul is not the body; the body houses the soul. If you know your Soul already, you know it appreciates love and attention. It speaks to you from the depths of the quiet. Listen to the deepest impulse within your being – and you will find your Soul.

The Soul needs to be fed, exercised and rested as well. To feed to Soul, allow yourself quiet time every morning before you turn on the computer or phone, before you check email or Facebook. Sit and allow your soul to catch up with our body. Meditation is a wonderful practice. Sitting outside and looking at nature does as much good for the soul. Drop your awareness out of your head and into your body, for it is in the body that you find the soul. Listen to uplifting music. Anything that causes your heart to swell is feeding the soul.

Exercise the Soul by visioning, dreaming and listening to it's still and quiet impulse. Read spiritual material that causes you to feel uplifted or contemplate. Think about what you know and why you know it. Could there be more to your story? Think about creation itself, and how it is ever evolving and your part in it.

Rest is vital to a healthy Soul. When your physical or mental body are tired, the soul suffers. Sit quietly. Bask. Enjoy the moment. Take naps. Laugh out loud, dance, be silly, giggle. Roll on the ground with a baby, toddler or your favorite pet. Let go of the boundaries of what you think you should be doing and simply be!

Our souls are our most precious commodity. They are resilient, brilliant, glorious, wise and creative, but if they are not cared for, you will experience burn out, stress and disappointment in life. Put the care and keeping of your Soul top on your list and you will be able to give and give without being drained.

Here are three practices or guidelines to saving your soul, while giving your all:

Do not work harder than your clients.

One particular client I had in my early days of coaching was so very close to a breakthrough. I could see it, I could taste it and she just wouldn't get there. I tried everything I knew and bunches of things I was making up in the process to help her to shift. I discovered one day, after months of working consistently with her that I was definitely working harder than her. She was coming to me for a pick me up, shot in the arm, make me feel better for a moment session, but not doing anything with it. Meanwhile, I'm doing all the work I think she needs to do and bending over backwards for her. In the moment I realized I was working harder than her, I quit.

I talked to her and set up new boundaries. I gave her concrete assignments between our sessions and told her I'd only see her after she'd done the homework. I let go of my attachment to being a success, to having her change in the way I thought was best for her and step into the potential I could see for her.

I realized my attachment and expectation was overriding what she was really wanting. She wanted a sounding board, each and every week.

She wanted to stay stuck in her victim mode and was unwilling to, at that moment anyway because I was doing all the work for her, to take responsibility for her life.

I don't want you to have to experience the same thing, so do not work harder than your clients.

Replenish Your Soul

Many coaches that are making the big bucks, who have a six-figure income and are rocking their work, experience such a sense of being out of balance. Recently, I asked a group of women, mostly coaches, if it would be alright if life got easier. Overwhelmingly, and resoundingly the answer was YES!

One woman that I've worked with went from a corporate job into her coaching practice and in the transition got into huge debt. So much that it was threatening her with bankruptcy. Within a couple of years, she was getting some clients and doing good work. Then one day, everything fell apart. The unbalance she was living in caught up with her. She was living on a fine edge and she tumbled over. Within a couple of days, a number of clients canceled their programs, a financial challenge came up and she was at the bottom of her bottom. She freaked out and had a very nice melt-down. Luckily for this woman, she had support all around her. She got into a program I was teaching at the time and turned her money around. She got busy and busier. She had one month where she received more income than she had the entire previous year. It looked like she had it all.

Fast forward a few months and this gal is rocking it! She is flying across the globe, attending phenomenal events, creating programs that are filling overnight and making three times what she's ever made in her life. She recently had a month that surpassed her entire previous year income wise. It's crazy good, right?

Right. Except her relationship fell apart and her fiancé broke up with her; her young son is missing his mama because she is so busy and pulled so many directions that she hardly has the energy for quality time with him. Even though most would say she is hugely successful financially, she says she feels worse than she ever has, she has gained extra weight and can't find time to exercise. She is definitely in an over-givers syndrome. Now, there is no judgement here, only learning for the rest of you.

Let's look at this as a coaches' syndrome. Our clients absolutely love us, our bank account is overflowing and bulging at its seams and our waitlist is growing every day. But at the end of the day, we are depleted where we used to be full. At the end of the day, we fall into bed exhausted and get up early to do it all again. When we finally get a few days off from client calls, we run off to another event and adventure. It sounds like the lifestyle of the rich and famous, but if your soul is suffering, it's not going to work for long. Burn out is just around the corner.

Believe me, I know it. I've done it too. It is a success syndrome. But is it true success? Or in giving our all, did we lose our soul?

Please take a moment here to contemplate this question. No matter where you are along your coaching journey, if you are trying to make your first $1000 or are well into the six figure place, how's your well-being?

We are here on the planet to give of ourselves, to bring our gifts forward and contribute to the world. We are here to experience ever increasing abundance, joy, life, healthy and expression. When we get out of balance our soul suffers.

My work is to bring balance, to find the path that works for you, the whole entire you. We can have six or seven figure incomes, or we can make a very measly amount, it doesn't really matter. What matters most is, are you happy? Truly happy? In your life, with the entirety of your life. Or is there something missing somewhere.

What could be missing?

Fun, adventure, quiet, intimacy, contentment, resting. These are the things I see most.

When you put your Soul first, you will be filled up and ready to give with healthy boundaries. It is not healthy to work 60 or 70 hours a week and then fall into a fitful sleep. It is healthier to take time every day to connect with your soul, to laugh and dance and play. Yes, every day!

We became entrepreneurs seeking a life style. Set it up early. Don't wait until later to add in the fun and soul feeding activities. Let it happen. Relax a little. Take a breath. Sit down with nothing in your hands or on your minds for at least 30 minutes each and every day. Let your soul breath, let your body rest and let your mind wander aimlessly in a dreaming, meandering, wandering state (as opposed to figuring things out, high alert state).

When I asked another group of women what their souls were yearning for, across the board they said, time and space to renew, to replenish, to relax with no demands on them. It is the gift that we seldom give ourselves. I encourage time away. I encourage what I call silent retreats. Taking a few days away, alone with no work. No creation of the next program, no planning or strategizing, but simply basking with yourself, your heart and soul. If you can't take time away, take 15 minutes every day to sit alone. In meditation, if that is easy and works for you, or with yourself. If you have family, taking a long bath can serve this purpose quite nicely. Even in the middle of the day, early morning or late at night before sleep.

Take time to replenish your soul. Sit still, without thought every day. There is a native American practice of sitting still several times a day. When asked why they do this the response is: We are waiting for the Soul to catch up with the body. Get out in nature, take a walk, do some yoga, put on some dance music in your office and move your body!

Put You first. Do something fun every day, find the things that bring you joy. Dancing, Singing, Spinning, laying out full on the floor. Do something creative every day, do some artistic play. Put color (paint, crayon, colored pencil, marker) on paper. Crank your favorite music and dance! Move your body! Take time to bask, live the life you want, relax, step away. If even for 10 minutes, make this a part of the day that you will not miss, no matter what!

As over givers, we tend to put ourselves last. This will not work in the long run of being a coach and entrepreneur. Set up your practice to include time for You; meditation, dance, movement, exercise, etc.

Time management becomes about taking care of You and what is most important, there will always been one more business thing you can do, especially on the internet. Your first!

Get support; join or create a group, so on those moments when you feel alone and like there is no one else out there, you know you aren't. Build relationships with colleagues early on. Become a support to someone else a few steps behind you.

Listen To The Impulse

Deep within the core of our being there is an impulse. It is life, it is creation, it is the souls' calling to the next expression. Listen deeply to your soul and the impulse. Our soul has that great and grand purpose that we mentioned earlier. Do you know what it is? Nurture it, develop it by spending time every day in a daydreaming mode asking yourself, what would I love?

What is your great grand vision? Do you know? Can you state it simply and clearly in a few sentences? If not, spend some time making it more concrete. Who would you be, what would you be doing, how would you be feeling if you were living the vision? Keep your dreams alive and in front of your awareness always. This helps to build a bridge from where you are to where you want to be. Having this anchored in your awareness helps keep your mind out of the minutia and on the bigger picture. It also creates an energetic frequency that all of creation will support you in achieving.

Listen deeply to what the impulse is calling you to be and then to do, not only for the great grand vision, but every moment of every day. Does it feel good and right to take this action now? Is there something else that would serve me better? Does this serve the greater purpose? Or is it distraction? Is it on purpose or busywork? As you get clear and follow your deeper wisdom, time opens up. Tasks get easier to complete and those that are not important drop away.

Get in touch with your WHY! Why do you do what you do? Why do you want what you want? Your Big Why is what gets you up in the morning and keeps you going when the going gets tough.

When you sincerely put yourself and your Soul first

and foremost the doorways of all your dreams open up. You will discover pathways that lead you to where you want to be with exciting adventures along the way. Connecting deeply with your Soul, will keep you in a balanced state of being. Being balanced is about flexibility and the ability to adjust in any moment. Think about balancing on one foot, the tree position in yoga. Although on the outer it might appear still, balance is about making those minute adjustments, using the tiny muscles to hold the course. Being balanced is never rigid, it is always fluid. As a coach, you will have times when life appears out of balance in a given day, you still have the opportunity to balance life over the next few days.

If we aren't careful we will give so much of ourselves away that we have nothing else to give, we risk being dried up, burned out and eventually no good to anyone else.

We all need to find a way to be balanced and nurtured and nourished along the way. It is not healthy to care more about our clients than we do about our own soul. Let's not do that! Saving your soul, while giving you all will bring to you a sense of peace, contentment and fulfillment, at each step along the journey called life.

I'd love to support you along your journey by inviting you into my private Facebook group here: www.bit.ly/findingease

Resources

Natural and Adaptive Styles Comparison

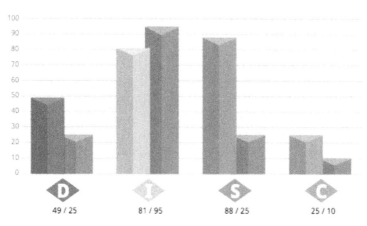

D	I	S	C
49 / 25	81 / 95	88 / 25	25 / 10

Patti O.eary

Natural Style:

The natural style is how you behave when you are being most natural. It is your basic style and the one you adopt when you are being authentic and true to yourself. It is also the style that you revert to when under stress or pressure. Behaving in this style, however, reduces your stress and tension and is comforting. When authentic to this style you will maximize your true potential more effectively.

Adaptive Style:

The adaptive style is how you behave when you feel you are being observed or how you behave when you are aware of your behavior. This style is less natural and less authentic for you or your true tendencies and preferences. When forced to adapt to this style for too long you may become stressed and less effective.

2

176

Executive Summary of Patti's Values

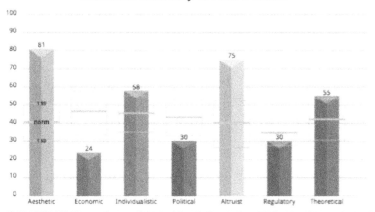

Very High Aesthetic	You place great importance in finding a good work-life balance, creating more than destroying and artistic self expression.
Low Economic	You are a team player and may put others' needs before self.
High Individualistic	You have no problem standing up for your own rights and may impart this energy into others as well.
Low Political	You are supportive of the efforts of the team; no hidden agendas. Willing to surrender control.
Very High Altruist	You have a very high sincerity-factor and a high empathy for others' needs.
Average Regulatory	You are able to balance and understand the need to have structure and order, but not paralyzed without it.
High Theoretical	You have a high interest level in understanding all aspects of a situation or subject.

5

177